CINCINNATI TURNER

SOCIETIES

THE CRADLE of an AMERICAN MOVEMENT

DANN WO

THE History PRESS

Published by The History Press
Charleston, SC 29403
www.historypress.net

Cover design by Natasha Walsh

Images are from the author's collection unless otherwise noted.

First published 2012

Manufactured in the United States

ISBN 978.1.60949.385.1

Library of Congress CIP data applied for.

Notice: The information in this book is true and complete to the best of our knowledge. It is offered without guarantee on the part of the author or The History Press. The author and The History Press disclaim all liability in connection with the use of this book.

To Roger, my father.

Contents

Preface

In Cincinnati, there remains a great deal of untranslated history about the German American community. There are wonderful stories waiting to be discovered in the Cincinnati German newspapers now on microfilm—like the *Volksfreund*, the *Volksblatt* and the *Freie Presse*. It has been my great pleasure to restore some of these wonderful firsthand accounts of the German American immigrants of Cincinnati who were Turners. These accounts offer pieces of a larger puzzle to be assembled as more scholars translate and publish these histories. The picture of the German American experience from the firsthand voices of these immigrants gives us a fresh perspective, describing how the distinct German social fabric of Cincinnati was woven.

The study of the German immigrant minority group, their trials and tribulations and their positive influences can give us new tools with which to coexist and value the current immigrant minority groups in America. The Cincinnati Turners were responsible for melting the early cultural frigidity of Cincinnati, recorded by early writers like Frances Trollope, under the warmth of their German *gemütlichkeit,* or joviality. The story of the Cincinnati Turners invigorates pride in our city's German American heritage and gives us a great legacy to promote to visitors of our beautiful city.

An old photograph of my great-grandfather, Theodore Ernst Woellert, sparked my interest in the Turners. The photo was taken for his 1884 wedding to Carolina Henke at Holy Trinity Church in Over-the-Rhine. A mysterious gold pin shone from his lapel. I was sure it held an interesting story that would connect me to my German immigrant ancestors in Cincinnati. I scanned the photo and enlarged the lapel for a better view. After researching several local German organizations, I came up with no leads—until I ran across the Cincinnati Turnverein.

In an old history of Cumminsville, the Cincinnati neighborhood where my ancestors settled, I discovered their Turnverein. I found a group photo of neighbors taken at the 1889 Cincinnati Bundesturnfest, a sort of German Olympics of other Turner associations in America. In the Cincinnati German newspaper articles recording the event, I found the exact oak leaf wreath symbol shown on my ancestor's lapel pin. In the oak leaf was intertwined the monogram "FFST," standing for "Frish, Frei, Stark, und Treu"—the motto of the American Turner organization at the time that means "Bold, Free, Strong, and Loyal." Now I had made the link to my German immigrant ancestors.

The more I researched the organization, the more I realized how similar my own nuclear family was to these early Turner families. I dove into the organization's history and began to understand the equal influences that my parents had taught me on fitness—physical and cultural. Sports and fitness were key parts of my father's DNA. He had latched on to a training manual of the Royal Canadian Air Force when we were in grade school, and even in his seventies, he still practices some exercises each morning. He was also a pool shark and an amateur baseball player, and he was famous for his aggressive return volleys in family volleyball games. He involved me, my brother, Tommy, and my sister, Jen, in a variety of sports from an early age. The motto of the high school that my father, my brother and I attended, "mens sana in corpora sano," or "sound mind in a sound body," is the motto of the American Turner Association. My mother rounded out our education by instilling an appreciation for the arts and dance. She had been a ballroom dancer in her early twenties and involved my sister in dance from an early age. Our family dinner table discussions involved ethics, morality and even my father's game of "Guess who owns this national brand," mirroring the Geistiges Turnen (Mental Debates) that the Turners promoted in their organization.

I even learned that the Marian Day activities that my Catholic grade school held in the 1980s were actually a conversion from the May Day athletic festivities that the Cincinnati Turners had introduced to Cincinnati public schools in the 1880s, consisting of games, dancing and sports. Gym activities that I practiced in grade school, like rope climbing and others, were designed by the Cincinnati Turners. Even one of my childhood favorites, kickball, was invented by a North Cincinnati Turner instructor. This connection inspired me to learn more about the origins of this little-known organization in Cincinnati. The result was a discovery of not only the wonderful Cincinnati Central Turner history but also a history of several associated Cincinnati and northern Kentucky neighborhood Turner Societies.

The Turners are arguably the most influential German social organization in the United States and the most patriotic of all immigrant groups. The German Turners adapted to their new Fatherland while preserving the traditions of their homeland. Turners were Renaissance men and women, artists, musicians, freethinkers, sharpshooters, athletes, gymnasts, intellectuals, writers, activists and patriots—all of whom were important in founding the strong urban centers of American cities before the industrial era. They tended to be anti-congregational in their religious thinking in the early years, but they opened their organization to all spiritual thinking. Their focus on mental and physical health influenced the progressive movement and the founding of important organizations like the YMCA, which adapted the Turner philosophy to its own organization. They were the driving force behind establishing physical education as an integral part of the American public school systems. They also founded and supported kindergartens and fought against slavery in the Civil War and for women's suffrage, labor rights, freedom of religion, freedom of the press and the separation of church and state.

They were different from other social groups in America at the time. Theirs was not a secret society like the Masons; they had no secret initiation processes. They only had to agree to exercise regularly and pursue a healthy spiritual and physical life free from prejudice. The Turners were and still are a fully integrated family social club, not excluding women or children from the society.

No other city in America, except Chicago, Illinois, has had as many offshoot neighborhood Turner Societies as the Cincinnati Turners. This speaks to both the importance of the Turner movement in the city of Cincinnati and to its large concentration of German Forty-eighter immigrants. In total, six offshoot neighborhood Turner Societies were supported in addition to the Central Turners in Over-the-Rhine: Cumminsville (1870–95), West End (1881–1910), North Cincinnati/Corryville (1881–1932), Lick Run (1881–88), the German-Hungarian Turners (1916–18) and the Norwood Turners (1905–38). Additionally, the area supported three other Greater Cincinnati Turner Societies in Newport (1852–1936), Dayton (1877–circa 1880) and Covington (1855–present) in northern Kentucky, right across the Ohio River. The

Covington Turners are still active today. Cincinnati Turners went on to found New Ulm, Indianapolis, Leavenworth and other Turner Societies in the United States. The formation of these societies followed the intracity migration of German immigrants, and their second- and third-generation descendants, as they moved to new German neighborhoods uphill from the downtown Cincinnati basin.

The Cincinnati Turners were also the most ambassadorial and conservative of all the American Turnvereine (Turner Societies) and acted for many years as the Mutterverein (Mother Society), guiding the constitutions and actions of the various national societies. It did not, as an organization, take rash action against issues. Although the members practiced free discussion and debate, they lobbied and negotiated smartly with government officials to spread their influence. They mediated between the socialist and radical Freethinker views for the good of the Cincinnati German community at large. They valued political discussion and the presentation of all sides, regardless of how liberal or socialist the views might be. They hosted lively discussions at the Turnhall of some individuals who might be considered radicals or infidels. In the end, they took a more conservative approach to fighting the issues of the days that affected the working German community of Cincinnati. They chose to preserve the peace with the Anglican majority of their new homeland, and they initiated more successful ways of lobbying. They helped to elect candidates to office who supported the views of the German American community, such as state senator and West End Turner Wilhem Steuve, presidents like William Howard Taft and Congressional representatives like Bellamy Storer, who voted for the interests of the German community in Cincinnati.

While Turner Societies tended to be conservative, some of the societies in other cities, particularly Indianapolis, called themselves Social Democratic or Socialer Turner Societies. That socialism, however, was more of a pre-Marxist type, being concerned mainly with securing better working conditions and wider public educational opportunities.

The Turner organization both locally and nationally has gone through a great deal of change and evolution over its more than 160 years of history, but the guiding principle of promoting a "sound mind and a sound body" still remains. This work will follow the evolution of the nation's first Turner Society and show the influence of the Turner principles in the making of our great nation.

I would like to thank Greg Mobely, archivist of the amazing American Turner Collection at the Indiana University School of Physical Edcucation; Margaret Linz, president of Cincinnati Central Turners; Lois Lynch and Mary Jane Dunning, of the Dayton Liederkranz Turners, for surrendering their wonderfully preserved Cincinnati Turner collection; Linda Houston and Max Ernst of the Covington Turners; Don Heinrich Tolzmann of the German American Cultural Museum; Dr. Carl Sputh II, grandson of Cumminsville Turner physical instructor Oscar Sputh; Jack Brendamour, great-grandson of Turner Edmund Brendamour, as well as his sons, Michael and Doug; Gary Lind, Lick Run and Martini church historian; Linda Bailey of the Cincinnati Historical Society; Joseph Reinhart, author of *A German Hurrah*, for his insight and encouragement; Jennifer of the Kentucky Historical Society; Denise West, curator of Chattanooga and Chickamauga National Military Park; Kevin Grace of University of Cincinnati Rare Books; Jenny French of the Walnut Hills Alumni Association; and Sherry Marshall of the Irma Tafel Boericke (sister of Gustav Tafel) Collection.

The Founding and the Antebellum Years

Liberty against all oppression.
—Turner constitution

The Napoleonic era (1799–1815) in Central Europe was an oppressive time for many Germanic people. A man named Friedrich Ludwig Jahn (1778–1852) began teaching gymnastics as a way to promote physical health, patriotism, readiness and resistance to the Napoleonic Empire. Fueled by the growing sense of nationalism for a united Germany, Jahn used sports to strengthen the will of the Germanic people to overthrow French domination by Napoleon. What we now refer to as Germany was until 1871 a loose confederation of principalities, duchies, kingdoms and city-states of people who shared only a similar common language. However, each area had its own dialect and social and gastronomic customs.

While the young United States was trying to fend off the British for the second time, Jahn started the first Turner Society in 1811 to espouse these tenets of physical health and mental readiness. In the Turner world, he would be lovingly referred to as "Turnvater" Jahn. He established the first outdoor gymnasium (turnplatz) for his club in the Hasenheide (Hare Meadow) outside Berlin, Germany, promoting organized competition. Five hundred young men and boys came to learn and practice his form of exercise. Jahn is also credited with inventing much of the gymnastics equipment still used today, like the parallel bars, the pommel horse and the flying rings. It was only four years after Jahn's founding of the first

Turnverein that the combined Germanic forces defeated Napoleon's armies at the Battle of Waterloo in Belgium.

Jahn's descendants continued to influence the American Turner movement when they immigrated to America in the 1850s, after the founding of the first Turnverein in Cincinnati. In the 1880s, the grandson of Friedrich Ludwig Jahn, Herman Heinrich Jahn, was a Turner instructor for the St. Louis Turnverein after graduating from the Turner Teacher's College (Turnlehrer Seminar) in Milwaukee, Wisconsin.[1] Jahn's great-great-great-grandson, Ernest John Rohr, was a U.S. senator for Illinois, born on May 12, 1963, in Chicago. In 1999, Ernest Rohr visited Germany on a tour, the first time a descendant of Jahn's had been back since Jahn's son, Arnold Siegfried Jahn, immigrated to Baltimore, Maryland, in 1852.[2]

The story of the Cincinnati Turner Society starts with another German immigrant who would become the pivotal man in the founding of the organization and the Father of the American Turner movement. That man was Friedrich Hecker. Hecker was born in Eichtersheim, in the Grand Duchy of Baden, appropriately enough, on September 28, 1811, the same year the first Turnverein was founded by Jahn. He was born the son of a wealthy court councilor of Prince-Primate von Dalberg. Hecker received his schooling at the Mannheim Gymnasium (High School) and studied law at the Universities of Heidelberg and Munich before receiving his doctorate in law at Heidelberg.[3]

Hecker then began practicing law as an advocate in Mannheim in 1838, one year before he married Marie Josephine Eisenhardt, daughter of a prominent Mannheim family. This "Mannheim Steamroller" became a politician in 1842, winning a seat in the district of Weinheim-Ladenburg in the lower chamber of the Baden State Assembly. Hecker made himself a prominent member of the liberal wing of the assembly, increasing his rock star prominence with dramatic speeches and theatrical displays aimed at gaining popular support.[4]

One such dramatic speech in 1845 gave Hecker particular political notoriety. In this inflammatory oration, he denounced the annexation of Schlieswig-Holstein in northern Germany to the Kingdom of Denmark. Through this criticism of the government of Baden and other Germanic states, Hecker became one of the most important leaders of the German Left movement before the outbreak of the general revolution in Europe in March 1848.[5]

Hecker paired up with socialist Gustav Strueve in calling an assembly of people at Offenburg on March 19, 1848, seeking to obtain the elimination of princely governments. After failing to obtain the support of the preliminary meeting of the German Parliament at Frankfurt, Hecker and Strueve called for an armed uprising on behalf of this new Unified German Republic on April 12. By April 20, they had aroused a small force that marched from Constance through the High Black Forest to the town of Kandern against the armies of Hesse and Baden, but they were defeated. The liberal coup was, however, able to kill the commander of the Baden and Hessian troops, General Friedrich von Gagern.[6] The credit for Gagern's killing was given to Herr Schoenberger, who after the failed revolution fled to Cincinnati, where he would reunite with Hecker during his short visit later that year.

As a result of this defeat, many liberal Germans immigrated to America to escape government persecution, with the idea to start a "new Germany" in America or to return when conditions were right. These brave, inspired men and their families started the first major wave of Germanic immigration to America and became known as the "Forty-eighters" or, in German, the *Achtundviersigers*. They were, in effect, defeated, exiled and still enflamed products of the 1848 and 1849 Republican uprisings in Germany. With not much else in their possession, these Forty-eighters carried with them as part of their "cultural steamer trunks" their love of physical fitness based on Jahn's Turner principles, as well as their voracious pursuit of the undeniable rights of the common man.

Not all Forty-eighters were Turners, nor were all American Turner members Forty-eighters. It is estimated that several hundred of these Forty-eighters immigrated to Cincinnati, many of whom were trained and active Turners and became founders and prominent members of the Cincinnati Turnverein. Some even fought for the Union during the Civil War. Considering that the Forty-eighters were only an estimated 1 percent of the total German immigrant population that migrated between 1848 and 1860, it is remarkable how such a small group was so influential in establishing and perpetuating German cultural traditions in America.[7]

The typical Forty-eighter was a male in his twenties, unmarried, in excellent physical condition, classically educated, politically enlightened and financially stable or coming from a family of means. Many were Turners in the Fatherland. The Forty-eighter also desired to return to Germany as soon as possible to join with the forces of revolution against the corrupt power of the Germanic provincial princes. Many of these Forty-eighters were students at various Germanic kingdom universities during the uprising and were similar to the war protesters of the Vietnam War era. They shared the same sense of protest at the corrupt government under which they were coming of age. It could be said that the Forty-eighters were the first true American hippies. In the same way we link the sexual revolution with the Vietnam-era hippies, we can link the American progressive movement to the German American Forty-eighters and their Turner Societies.

When they settled in America, Forty-eighters sought professions that would exert influence on German American thought and practice. Many became proprietors of German-language newspapers that they used as vehicles to express their political views. Of a sample of biographies of three hundred Forty-eighters, roughly two-thirds held the profession of one of the following: journalist, physician, teacher, lawyer, businessman and author—all incredibly influential positions within their immigrant communities.[8]

After the loss at the Battle of Kandern, Hecker fled to Switzerland and then left for America in September 1848 after failed attempts to orchestrate further revolt. Three other 1848 revolutionists (who were also Turner gymnasts) from Ludwigsburg in the German state of Württemberg arrived in Cincinnati on October 11, 1848: J.A. Eiselein, Gottlieb Wiest and Carl Sprandel. They made their headquarters temporarily with Hecker's fellow countryman and friend from Rappenau in Baden, Leopold Kienzel (1796–1849), at the corner of Plum and Fifteenth Streets in Cincinnati's Over-the-Rhine, a heavily German neighborhood. Kienzel's daughter, Charlotte, would marry Cincinnati Turner Johann Lenhardt Schrieber (1829–1910), the fencing instructor for the club and later Cincinnati's leading cast-iron storefront manufacturer. Eiselein would eventually rent a third-floor room above the woodturning shop (*dreschlerei*) of Franz Hellferich. Hellferich operated a tavern next to his woodturning shop that was very popular with the young Forty-eighter immigrants.[9]

Hecker arrived in Cincinnati, Ohio, on October 22, 1848, five days after his steamboat was stuck on a sandbar in the Ohio River between Wheeling, West Virginia, and Cincinnati, Ohio. He was received with great fanfare by Cincinnati's German immigrant community with a torchlight parade in Over-the-Rhine. Although he had been given a letter of introduction to Timothy Walker, a wealthy Anglo Cincinnatian, and though a nice room had been prepared for him by the reception committee at the Broadway Hotel, he preferred to stay out of sight and with his own people at Carl Rebstock's German tavern called Zum Rebstock on the northwest corner of Vine and Fifteenth Streets in Over-the-Rhine.[10]

Although he wanted to stay out of the public eye, word spread quickly of his arrival, and he was visited by his many Forty-eighter refugee friends in Cincinnati at Zum Rebstock. Hecker and his friend Schoeninger, who

This is an advertisement in the November 22, 1848 *Cincinnati Volksblatt* for Zum Rebstock, the German guesthouse owned by Carl Rebstock; Friedrich Hecker stayed there in Cincinnati, and it was the first meeting place of the Cincinnati Turner Society.

was the celebrated killer of German general Friedrich von Gagern at the Battle of Kandern, spoke to those gathered to rousing cheers. Hecker had no intent on settling in Cincinnati; rather, he wanted to gather Forty-eighters together for fundraising to support another uprising in Germany against the monarchies. He made it known that he had plans to go to New York and Philadelphia in the next few days to rouse more support. Despite his quick stay, his words warmed the crowds. The editors of the *Volksblatt* met and interviewed Hecker at Zum Rebstock, noting that "he is a simple and gracious man. His efforts to support the German Revolution are not artificial or for personal gain, but come from a genuine love of his people."[11]

The next day, October 23, 1848, Kienzel, the owner of the tavern Hecker Haus, renamed in honor of Hecker's arrival, gave him an afternoon reception. After the reception, in the midst of other groups looking to procure an audience with Hecker, the Ludwigsburger immigrants (Eiselein, Wiest, Sprandel and Carl Leopold Fettweis), the Tafel brothers (Rudolf, Gustav and Albert) and Wilhelm Pfaender spoke with Hecker about the practicality of founding a gymnastic or Turner Society in Cincinnati.[12] The Tafel brothers' father, Leonhard Tafel, had founded a Turnverein in Schorndorf, Germany, and had been jailed for his outspokenness against the monarchy, so the Turner principles were part of the Tafel family's DNA.

Hecker ardently approved of this concept—to him the Turner Society was "the carrier, developer, and apostle of the free spirit," the same philosophy of the 1848 revolution. It would also give his fundraising operation a coherent group with which to organize more events to support another uprising in Germany. A Turner group that exercised, drilled, marched and sang patriotic German songs would give a very visible and tangible reminder to Cincinnati's Germanic immigrants of the lost fight back home. It would be like a living commercial for the ideals of the revolution.

An evening reception was given for Hecker at Zum Hirsch, the guesthouse of Mr. Faber. Graced by the voices of the German Liedertafel and the Arbeiter Singing Society, another torchlight parade was given for Hecker. Thousands of Cincinnati Germans gathered, visibly moving Hecker, especially when they sang "Long Live the German Republic" and "What Is the German Fatherland?" Hecker thanked the Cincinnati Germans for his warm reception, and Schoeninger spoke a few patriotic words. The *Volksblatt* noted that "the day will soon appear, where the glorious work Hecker started will be complete, and the banner of freedom of a united Germany will fly." That would indeed happen twenty-three years later, under Otto von Bismarck in 1871.[13]

Nearly a week later, on Thursday evening, November 2, 1848, in Carl Leopold Fettweis's rented rooms in the rear of the house of an old German immigrant named "Papa" Kloepper, on the corner of Thirteenth Street and Boots Alley (near today's Cincinnati hipster hangout, Tucker's Restaurant), the very first meeting of the Cincinnati Turnverein, the first continually operating Turner Society in America, commenced. Perhaps toasting with mugs of Cincinnati lager and singing patriotic songs, a committee was named to draft the Cincinnati Turner constitution. The German immigrants present at the meeting were J.A. Eiselein, Carl Leopold Fettweis, Wilhelm Pfaender, Carl Sprandel and Hugo Gollmer, as well as brothers Rudolph, Gustav and Albert Tafel. Almost two weeks later, on Tuesday, November 14, these men and some more who had been recruited met in Eiselein's third-floor room over Hellfereich's *dreschlerei* and tavern on the north side of Thirteenth Street opposite Jackson Street to discuss the draft constitution.[14]

The Cincinnati Turner Constitution was approved eight days later on November 21, 1848, at Kienzel's Hecker Haus on the corner of Plum and Canal Streets. This is the official date celebrated for the founding of the Cincinnati Turnverein. Officers were temporarily elected: Wilhelm Pfaender was *sprecher*, or president; Gustav Tafel was *schriftwart*, or secretary; Gottlieb Wiest was *kassier*, or treasurer; and C.L. Fettweis was Turnwart, or gymnastic director. The following members were accepted into the first Turner Society in America in Cincinnati: Otto Krebs; Adolph Krebs; C. Leopold Fettweis; Carl Sprandel; J.A. Eiselein; the brothers Rudolph, Gustav and Albert Tafel; Hugo Gollmer; Ferdinand Hoffmeister; Gottlieb Wiest; Wilhelm Pfaender; and the first *zoeglings* (boy Turners) in America, the young Tafel brothers, Hugo and Richard Tafel.[15]

Other members would quickly join that first year as the news of the new Cincinnati Turner Society spread: Mr. Gramer, Emil Krais, K.E. Portier, Louis Laile, Fritz Schneider, Phil Guettler, Fredrick Peter, August Wild, John Eggers, Mr. Lamarsky, H. Michfeld, August Hoffmeister, Heinrich Esmann, William Doll, George Poetz, Joseph Hoch, Andre Mueller, Karl Raab, A. Geisele, Emil Geisele, Georg Harar, George Graham, J. Hoffman and brothers Gustav, Adolph and Louis Authenreith.[16]

Hecker left Cincinnati for St. Louis the afternoon of October 24, right after he roused the immigrant Forty-eighters in Cincinnati and inspired the creation of the Cincinnati Turner Society, the first of its kind in America. But by the end of November 1848, Hecker appeared in New York City. Pairing with his Forty-eighter friend Gustav Strueve, he and others met in Louis Becker's Hotel in Hoboken, New Jersey, to found the New York Socialer Turnverein.[17] The Turner movement quickly spread throughout the nation; by 1851, there were 22 individual Turnvereine, with a combined membership of roughly 1,500. A National Turnerbund, or Association of Turner Societies, was also formed. By 1853, 70 Turnvereine had been formed, representing nearly every major city at the time. By 1860, when the Forty-eighter immigration had really ended, there were 157 Turner Societies, representing roughly 10,000 members, all connected politically and socially.[18]

Hecker settled in America in 1849, becoming a "Latin Farmer," a title comically given to the well-educated Forty-eighters who had no experience in agriculture before practicing it in America. He grew grapes on farms in Lebanon and Summerfield, Illinois. He also earned a steady income from speaking publicly in German and English, but he never held any major political office. In the Civil War, Hecker commanded the short-lived, all-German Twenty-fourth Illinois Volunteer Regiment and, later, the Eighty-second Illinois Volunteer Regiment, but he resigned in protest against mistreatment by his Anglo-American commanders during the Battle of Lookout Mountain, Tennessee. After the war, Hecker continued to speak in Republican circles and was an active columnist in the German press. He applauded the unification of the Germanic states in 1871 and even made a speaking tour of Germany in 1873, during which he achieved a legendary status. During his life, Hecker was ardently anti-clerical and anti-Catholic and hostile to prohibition.[19]

In 1883, two years after his death, the Cincinnati Turners dedicated a monument to their hero, Friedrich Hecker, in honor of helping to found the Cincinnati Turnverein and thus the American Turner movement.

The Friedrich Hecker monument was dedicated in Washington Park in Cincinnati's Over-the-Rhine neighborhood in 1883 to honor the hero of the German revolution of 1848 who helped to form the Cincinnati Turnverein.

The monument was erected in Washington Park, the equivalent of New York's Central Park to the Over-the-Rhine German community in Cincinnati. Washington Park had been founded in 1861 and was a center for social gatherings for the Cincinnati German community. Featuring a prominent bust of Hecker crafted by Cincinnati Turner sculptor Leopold Fettweis Jr., the monument features a shiller limestone and a gray granite base. Inscribed on the base of the Hecker Memorial are the German words "Mit Wort und That für Volksfreiheit im alten und neuen Vaterlande," which means, "With Word and Deed for the Freedom of the People in the Old and New Fatherlands."[20]

Franz Hellferich, the man who boarded J.A. Eiselein, one of the fourteen founders, donated an open lot next to his woodturning shop at Thirteenth and Jackson Streets, near today's Art Academy of Cincinnati, for the first Cincinnati turnplatz, or exercise field. They drilled in the yard with rifles and wands. Numerous and sometimes unfriendly crowds soon came to view the "outlandish spectacle" of their drilling, so they built a high board fence around the yard for privacy. The organization continued to grow. In 1850, the Cincinnati Turners had 150 members and grew to 222 members in 1851. Due to this large growth in membership, a suitable gymnasium was built. This small building was completed in 1851 on Jackson Street. At the dedication ceremony, Turner president Wilhelm Pfaender addressed those gathered. The Turner Maennerchor sang musical numbers, and a gymnastics competition was held and the winners awarded prizes by the ladies.[21]

The Cincinnati Turners and their public displays of gymnastics were getting great press and notoriety. Most non-Germans poked fun at these "White Jackets" and their Turnfests, but some progressives realized and

This is the first Turnhall of the Cincinnati Central Turners, built in 1851 and occupied until 1859. *Courtesy of Cincinnati Central Turners.*

accepted the benefits of regular exercise. One such progressive, Dr. Chrisin, founded America's first non-German Turnverein in Oxford, Ohio. Along with Mr. Roemmler as Turner instructor, the Oxford Turners were made up of 150 students at Miami University. On June 28, 1858, the Oxford Ohio Turners hosted a Turnfest in Oxford, Ohio, to show off the prowess of their new organization. They exhibited pyramid building and fencing, along with song and music, and William M. Corry from Cincinnati gave a speech.[22]

The Cincinnati Central Turnhall housed important gatherings of Germanic immigrants. On February 14, 1852, it housed a general meeting of Cincinnati German immigrants to listen to Hungarian revolutionary leader Louis Kossuth and Germanic revolutionary leader and poet Gottfried Kinkel. Kinkel had undertaken a fundraising tour through America to fund a revived German revolution, and Kossuth was doing the same for the Hungarian cause. The two would travel next to Indianapolis.[23]

A month after Kinkel and Kossuth lectured at the Cincinnati Turnhall, a German woman spoke there: Mathilde Franziska Anneke (1817–1884), a Forty-eighter suffragette who had immigrated to America with her husband because of their revolutionary activities. Anneke lectured on the newly forming suffrage movement and the rights of women. Although she and her husband were still in Europe during the 1848 Seneca Falls Conference, Anneke became part of the mainstream American suffrage movement in 1853 when she spoke at the Women's Rights Convention in New York. Her *Deutsche Frauen-Zeitung*, or *German Women's Newspaper*, which appeared in March 1852 in Milwaukee, Wisconsin, was the first feminist paper published by a woman in the United States, and it was used as a tool by Germanic women to educate themselves about the suffrage movement. A letter chronicles her 1852 speeches at the Cincinnati Turnhall:

> *After a dangerous trip of several days and nights through the Alleghanies, I reached Cincinnati where Gottfried Kinkel had just stirred the German element. Here in the Turnhall an exceedingly large audience received me, and I won lively applause for my always decidedly outspoken demands. I gave several lectures here and then turned to Louisville.*[24]

The Cincinnati Turners acted as ambassadors to their newly formed brother Turner Societies. On April 29, 1854, the Cincinnati Turner Singing Society gathered with delegates from Terre Haute, Lafayette, Madison, New Albany and Logansport, as well as from Shelbyville, Indiana, and Louisville, Kentucky,[25] for the consecration of the banner of the Indianapolis Turnverein. Cincinnati Turners led by Gustav Tafel returned in 1867 for the dedication of Indianapolis's new Turnhall. Tafel praised its new innovation of banning the bar from the Turnhall, something that would have been impossible to implement in Cincinnati.[26]

The Turnhall at 513–519 Walnut Street was built in 1859 for a cost of $35,000 under the direction of Karl Victor Beckmann. It was three stories high, had a red brick façade and was topped with a Greek lyre on the roof apex. The foundation was laid in May 1858, and it was dedicated on December 4, 1859, with an inspiring address by Gustav Tafel on New Year's Day 1860. The ground-floor rooms were rented to a variety of businesses over the years. The rear of the complex housed the gym, with parallel bars, swinging bars and a space for military drill.[27] Alterations would be made to this building in 1874, 1893, 1900 and 1948, but for nearly one hundred years, this was mission control for Cincinnati Germanic immigrants.[28]

The Cincinnati Turners reflected the lifestyle of a people who sought to preserve their cultural ties while being passionately involved in their new country. After the 1848 and 1849 revolutions in Germany fizzled without success, the Cincinnati German immigrant community became more committed to its new homeland, as well as to implementing the same

Mission control for the Cincinnati Turners: the 1859 Turnhall on Walnut Street. *Courtesy of Don Prout.*

cultural institutions it had enjoyed in Germany. People busied themselves with America, beginning to learn something about American history and politics and study the Constitution of the United States. The Forty-eighters and Turners discovered that in this best of all republics, there was still a great deal that was not right and an enormous amount that was very much in need of improvement. While placing their liberal "loupe" on the Constitution, they found the American condition to be a mass of incoherencies and contradictions and felt that all these crying injustices needed reform.

While upholding their German ancestry, the Cincinnati Turners were very patriotic to their new country. Most Turner Society constitutions required a member to be a citizen of the United States or at least be in the process of obtaining U.S. citizenship. The North American Turner Records recorded yearly the number of U.S. citizens in its membership rolls in all national organizations.

A volunteer militia had been founded in 1848 in Cincinnati, with the goal of helping its brothers fight the revolution back in Europe. That organization became a casualty of the end of the 1848 revolution, but it left behind a beautiful unfinished flag with the president of the Turner Damenverein (Ladies Society), Mrs. Emil Klauprecht. The president of the Cincinnati Turners at the time, Professor Heinrich Eismann, and Emil Klauprecht, a

Turner and editor of the *Wochenblatt*, encouraged the modification of this flag as the emblem for their own organization. An oak leaf and snake on the flag suited the Turners. Hugo Gollmer's mother, Catherine—sort of the "Betsy Ross" of the organization—completed the needlework on the flag, and John Deirelein gilded the eagle on the flag. So, on November 5, 1850, the women and girls of the Cincinnati Turners presented their handmade black, red and gold flag of the Cincinnati Turner Society, the colors of the 1848 revolution and the German Republic, wedding the society to the ideals of a united Germanic people.[29]

A firsthand account of the event is taken from the diary of Pauline Authenreith Tafel, a member of the Damenverein and daughter of Ferdinand Friedrich Authenreith, a Forty-eighter immigrant to Cincinnati from Stuttgart: "The dedication was a great event. I as president surrounded by twelve sister members made the presentation. The following afternoon the Turners marched past our house and saluted me with cheers. That was the first flag borne publicly in Cincinnati by a German Club."[30]

The elder Authenreith had owned a bookstore in Stuttgart, Germany, and had written political articles for the *Fliegende Blatter*. When he lampooned a German monarch in a poem in one of his articles, his friends recommended that he immigrate to America to escape persecution. So Ferdinand Authenreith, his wife and their ten children immigrated to Cincinnati in 1849. The three oldest brothers—Gustav, Louis and Adolf—became first-year members of the Turner Society in 1849. Their sister Pauline gave an account of that first year in the Turner organization:

> *This* [the Turnverein] *gave our lives some diversion, although every evening we were uneasy until the brothers were safe at home, for the bright Turner uniform was a thorn in the side of the American youth. The Turners were often persecuted with stoning so that they had to take the side streets. Nonetheless, the club grew quickly and during the winter we already enjoyed agreeable social contacts. On Sunday afternoons we came together, drank coffee or something else. Whoever could recite anything or sing, did so. During the spring of 1850 a hall had to be rented; gymnastics were practiced in a space partitioned by boards...The turners began now to flourish and grow. Whenever a Sunday morning promised fair weather we would set out bright and early with laughter and song and to the tune of "Lustigen Musikanten" march to the woods or to Longworth's Wine Garden. By and by the Turners were regarded with more esteem although they still had to contend with obstacles.*[31]

Given the German propensity toward singing, especially when accompanied with drink, Turner Saengvereine, or singing societies, were soon formed, as were Turner literary societies. The Turnhall housed a German-language library that was sort of a reading room for the German American literati in Cincinnati. Men could use the library to read local German newspapers and German classical authors like Goethe. The very first Saengerbund formed of many Cincinnati singing societies, including the Turner Maennerchor, was formed in Cincinnati in 1849. The large number of these German singing societies in Cincinnati spawned the first Saengerfest (Singing Festival) in the city in 1851 and, later, in 1873, the Cincinnati May Festivals, both led by groups of Turner singers. It's this long legacy of singing that landed Cincinnati the honor of hosting the 2012 World Choir Games.

The *Turnzeitung* (the Turner national newspaper), the first of its kind in the United States, was started in Cincinnati in January 1851 by Heinrich Essman, who was president of the Cincinnati Turners for many of the early years. After only ten issues, the publication was taken over by the newly organized Turner Bund, formed in October 1851 in Philadelphia by Turner members from New York, Boston, Brooklyn and Baltimore. Wilhelm Rapp, writing in the *Turnzeitung*, declared that the objective of the Turnvereine should be a quest for political, social and religious reform.[32]

On September 1, 1853, the Shützenverein (Shooting Society) of the Cincinnati Turners was founded. Members' parading through the streets of Over-the-Rhine gave rise to suspicion and indignation among nativists. Several Cincinnati Turners were gunsmiths and supplied the Turners with rifles, many of which were brought along with the Ninth Ohio to fight in the Civil War. Anton Kutzleb—one of the early *zoeglings*, or child Turner pupils, of Friedrich Bertsch—manufactured guns before the Civil War. Henry L. Seibert also made guns in the 1850s and operated the Buckeye Gun Store at 230 Main Street.[33]

A music corps was founded in 1854 by Albin Stecher and Joseph Boehm that would become one of the most cherished groups in the organization.[34] It led Turner parades, Turner funeral processions and even the Ninth Ohio Volunteers in the Civil War, as well as entertained at Turner celebrations.

Each Turner member received his own card. This served as a passport that could earn a card-carrying member a free stay at any Turnhall from Boston, Massachusetts, to Sacramento, California, as well as an instant letter of recommendation into any German community in the United States. As many of the early Turners moved frequently between cities, this card became very handy.

This is the 1854 Turner membership card of Herman Franz Erd. The card served as an instant letter of introduction in any city in the United States. *Courtesy of Brown County Minnesota Historical Society.*

Cincinnati Turners retained influence on the national level. Heinrich Esmann, president of Cincinnati Turners, was also national president from 1855 to 1856, followed by one of the founders, Albert Tafel, from 1856 to 1858.[35]

Two wonderful lithographs from 1858 and 1861 document the early members and the variety of their activities and professions. The first print, titled *Turnleben in Cincinnati* ("Turner Life in Cincinnati"), shows an intimate group portrait of seventy-four members of the Cincinnati Turnverein standing on the Covington side of the Ohio River, with downtown Cincinnati in the background. Each portrait is based on a photograph and is keyed to his name below the image. A variety of activities are represented, including sharpshooting, gymnastics, singing, writing and even beer brewing and winemaking. Several musicians are shown with their instruments—a drum, a violin, guitars, dulcimers and a trumpet. The signature Turner white gymnast uniforms with black cravats are shown, along with beaded Turner belts, some with the Turner greeting "Gut Heil!" ("Good Health!"). The society flag—a red, gold and black flag, dated 1850—is shown, and a picture of the first Turnhall is seen at the bottom of the lithograph, with a motto below: "Durch Uebung zur Kraft, durch Kampf zum Licht," meaning, "Achieve strength through practice, enlightenment through struggle." A variety of men holding beer steins, drinking horns and wine glasses is shown. A Turner gymnastic formation is shown on the middle right, as well as a father and son and even a man with his greyhound dog.

The second lithograph, titled *Cincinnati Turner*, was printed in 1861 just before the outbreak of the Civil War. The new, larger Turnhall is shown in the legend. It is again keyed with members' names and shows a variety of activities, not forgetting a tapped keg of beer surrounded by stein-bearing members. Also shown are three young boys and two young girls. The Cincinnati Turners had already started classes for young boys and girls in 1855, preceding the national Turner resolution requiring it in 1856.

A group of four men is shown with their fencing swords. The man to the left with his sword in a lunge is a young Johann Leonhardt Schreiber. He was married to Kienzel's daughter, Charlotte. In addition to manufacturing fencing swords for the society, he also manufactured bayonet knives for the Turner members who volunteered in the Ninth Ohio Volunteer Infantry during the Civil War. He was the fechtwart (fencing instructor) for the

This 1858 lithograph, titled *Turnleben in Cincinnati*, was drawn by Turner Friedrich Bertsch and printed by Ehrgott & Forbriger. It depicts a Turner outing on the Kentucky side of the Ohio River, with Cincinnati in the background. *Courtesy of Cincinnati Central Turners.*

This 1861 lithograph by Ehrgott & Forbriger is titled *Cincinnati Turner* and provides a pre–Civil War view of the Cincinnati Turnverein. *Courtesy of Cincinnati Central Turners.*

Turners for more than thirty years. He won many prizes, including the fencing trophy at the 1855 Cincinnati National Turnfest. In 1861, he incorporated Schreiber & Sons Ironworks on Walnut Street, which supplied cast-iron storefronts, many still visible in Over-the-Rhine, to locations as far away as Texas, Chicago and New York.[36]

The early Cincinnati Turners took great pride in their organization. Adam Dilg (1813–1875), born in Hesse and a Turner since January 1852, showed this Turner pride in the instructions in his will. He noted that he was no longer going to shave and go to church until he died, and he wanted to be buried in a coffin with a glass window, allowing his Turner pants to be visible. He wanted his eulogy to be given by Gustav Tafel or Moritz Jacobi, both early presidents of the Cincinnati Turners.[37]

In addition to the elected offices of president, vice-president, secretary, cashier and physical instructor, the barkeep was also an elected and highly coveted office. Every event of the Turners included either passing the drinking horn or tapping the keg. As a result, the Turnhall bar was a very profitable funder for the organization. In a Turner meeting in May 1861,

Above: Leonhardt Schreiber with his fencing sword. Next to him is Albert Seiter (with a confident smirk), holding his fencing sword but also with his sleeves rolled up to expose his muscular forearms, of which he was obviously very proud. *Courtesy of Cincinnati Central Turners.*

Left: A close-up from the 1861 *Cincinnati Turner* lithograph of Adam Dilg holding a stein of local Cincinnati lager with his arm around his young daughter, Ada Dilg, the first known American representation of an *activ Turner madchen*, or active Turner girl. *Courtesy of Cincinnati Central Turners.*

they reported the staggering bar earnings of $1,000 to date for the year. Adolph Sieter was barkeep at the time but apparently fell short of his duties, as Mr. Reinkenberger was elected barkeep at a meeting on May 11, 1861.[38]

Cincinnati Turners Friedrich Bertsch and Christian Bohlaender formed the first children's Turner school or Knabenturnschule (class for adolescent boys) in America on June 1, 1855. On August 5, 1855, they opened the first Turner classes in the country for young and teenage girls. On September 23, 1855, they opened the first Zoeglingsverein (class for preadolescent boys). In the first year, there were 255 boys in the school, and the next year, there were a total of 385 students—40 pre-adolescent boys, 280 adolescent boys and 65 girls.[39]

This Turner-adopted concept of early childhood education and activity was a unique concept for pre–Civil War child rearing in the United States. These activities proved to be very beneficial to these sons and daughters of early German immigrants, building their confidence and fostering their talents.

One early member of the child Turner class, Ludwig Schimpf, born in 1853 in Cincinnati to immigrant parents, became the first child president of his class and distinguished himself in competition at local and national Turnfests. Class instructor Friedrich Bertsch, who also operated a drawing school for the children free of charge, noticed that he had talent in painting and drawing and influenced him to be sent to the Art Academy, which set him up for a lifelong career in the interior design business for Cincinnati's wealthy Germans.[40] Another first member of the child Turner class, Wilhelm Authenreith, went on to found a medical instruments company and was treasurer of the Turner Building and Loan for more than twenty years.

Following the lead of the Mother Society and the American Turner Convention of 1856, a resolution was offered to instruct young boys and girls. Before this time, with the exception of the Cincinnati Turnverein, only men and teenage boys were instructed.

Constantin Conrad, a former Cincinnati Turner who relocated to Pittsburgh, Pennsylvania, took the concept of starting Turner classes for young boys and girls with him and founded in 1860 the first such classes at the Pittsburgh Turnverein. Even though girls were allowed to be instructed, it wouldn't be until the Louisville, Kentucky Turnfest of 1921 that women were allowed to compete in national Turnfests.[41]

The Turners took active participation very seriously. All members under thirty were required to attend every class and meeting night. If absent without excuse, members appeared before the board of directors to receive reprimand. On November 14, 1857, thirty members were expelled for neglect of attendance. In 1861, August Frey was expelled for playing billiards on a class night.[42]

September in Cincinnati seemed to be the best weather for hosting outdoor sporting events in the 1850s. On September 25, 1852, Cincinnati held its first Bundesturnfest (national Turnfest), and a short three years later, during September 15–19, 1855, Cincinnati hosted another. The Cincinnati active men's class and the children's class took the most prizes of any Turnvereine at the St. Louis, Missouri Turnfest, held from June 30 to July 5, 1860.

The 1850s were not an easy time for the Cincinnati Turners or the city's German immigrants. In dealing with a new homeland and a new language, as well as starting new careers, they had to deal with the prevalent nativism or anti-immigration against themselves propagated by the American Know-Nothing Party. In the 1848 *Cincinnati Volksblatt*, every edition from October through December had an article about the nativism experienced by the Cincinnati German immigrant community. Turners were nicknamed the "White Jackets" by the members of the Know-Nothing Party because of the white gymnastic uniforms they wore in exercises and at Turnfests.

The first decade in the life of the Cincinnati Turners was a time of great challenge. The influx in the 1850s of immigrants from Germany and Ireland sparked the rise of the nativist or Know-Nothing movement in America. The Know-Nothing political party was concerned with the growing numbers of Catholic and German-speaking people in the United States. Its name came from members responding with "I know nothing" when asked about their activities. They sought to limit the number of immigrants allowed in the United States and deny these immigrants the right to vote. The Cincinnati Turners and other Turners in America worked against the Know-Nothing Party, and often bloody clashes between them occurred in cities all over the United States, especially at election time and during Turnfests.

While the Turners defended themselves from anti-immigrant violence, they did not create sensational disturbances like the other large Cincinnati German organization, the *Freimaenner* or Freethinkers. The Freethinkers were made up of the more radical Forty-eighters who were extremely anti-clerical and advocated rationalism, science and history as proper guides for living, as well as criticized established religions for promoting superstition and bigotry. Although the Turners shared many of these views to a degree, they did not share the radical outspokenness of the Freethinkers.

When news reached Cincinnati in December 1855 that Cardinal Gaetano Bedini, the emissary to Pope Pius IX, would visit the city, the Freethinkers planned a hostile demonstration. They identified Bedini with the forces of oppression of the 1848 revolution in Germanic Europe. While the Cincinnati Turners refused to be a part of this "useless and untimely" movement, the Freethinkers joined wholeheartedly. They staged a procession to the residence of the Cincinnati Catholic archbishop John Purcell and burned Bedini in effigy. Carrying signs and bearing various anti-clerical slogans, about four hundred Germans, mostly Freethinkers, joined the march. The procession ended with force by the Cincinnati police: one protestor was killed, fifteen protestors were wounded and sixty were arrested. The event became known as the *Weihnacts Schlacht*, or Christmas Riot.

The first of these clashes involving the Cincinnati Turners occurred in April 1855 when the Know-Nothings nominated a slate of candidates, with James Taylor, the populist anti-immigrant editor of the *Cincinnati Times*, as candidate for mayor. Taylor's inflammatory attacks on immigrants inflated tension in the city, with fighting breaking out on election day. The day after, a mob of nativists attacked the German Over-the-Rhine neighborhood, causing a riot in which several men died. The nativist mob managed to destroy the ballots in two German wards. The Germans organized into militia units (including a Turner regiment), built a barricade across Vine Street and successfully defended their territory, even shooting their cannons over the heads of the nativist mob.[43]

Cincinnati Turners read in the *Cincinnati Volksfreund* that on July 4, 1855, their brother Turners in Columbus, Ohio, were again assaulted by nativists while parading back to the Turnhall after a picnic at Stewart's Grove—this time with stones and pistol shots. The Columbus Turners had been attacked by nativists that May on a canal bridge after a Pentecost Monday celebration, resulting in their defeat, with heads bloodied by stones. This time, one young man attacked the Turners while they were parading to their Turnhall and firing ensued, resulting in many injured and one death. Their physical instructor took a serious wound to the forehead.[44] As a result of this anti-nativism, the Columbus Turners disbanded for more than ten years. One month later, a similar anti-immigrant riot in the German wards of Louisville, Kentucky, affecting the Turner population there, occurred on August 6, 1855.[45]

One very violent nativist attack on the Cincinnati, Newport and Covington Turners occurred in May 1856 in Kentucky and became known as the *Pfingstmontag* (Pentecost Monday) Riot. The Turners of Covington invited the Newport and Cincinnati Turners to Forest Hill Park to dedicate the new Covington Turner Flag, made by their Women's Auxiliary. The event was celebrated with gymnastic exercises, target shooting, dancing and, of course, drinking. During the event, several young Anglo-American teenagers from Covington caused a scene at the beer stand, one of them wielding a knife. The knife was seized by one of the Turners, and the group was promptly escorted out of the festival by two rapier-armed Turners to avoid further violence. As the Turners were escorting this group of teenagers away from the picnic, a group on horseback questioned their intentions with the boys. When the boys reached Covington, they spread a rumor that the Turners had tried to kill all of them.

Sensing trouble brewing, the Turners decided to end their picnic early so that all the visitors could reach the Ohio River ferry at Newport before dark. The Turner group marched back to Covington in parade formation, with the band playing German songs and the women and children surrounded by armed Turners. As soon as the Turners exited Forest Hill, they were met with a shower of stones from rowdy teenagers and others they had gathered. One of the rowdies broke through the line of the parade and tried to steal the flag of the Junior Turner Society out of the hands of the flag carrier. But the Junior Turners fought back, giving the rowdies a sound whipping with their steel wands and rapiers. As they neared Covington, the mob on both sides of the streets increased, yelling threats and insults at the Turners, but they held formation.

As they continued marching, a well-known marshal of the Know-Nothing Party, Clinton Butts, tried to drag a Turner out of the formation to arrest him and was wounded on the shoulder; another of the mob, Marshall Harvey, was severely injured in the skull. Several Turners were also injured. The Turners proceeded across the Licking River Bridge to head to the Newport ferry so that the women and children could reach Cincinnati in safety, but the mob prevented the ferry from docking in Kentucky. Threats like "Kill the Dutchmen" were heard from the mob because the Turners would not surrender their arms. Turner captain Fred Miller led one group of sharpshooters, while Cincinnati Turner Fred Bertsch led the other group. Other Turners armed with their exercise tools—Indian clubs, rapiers and wands—were led by instructors Karl Roos and Wiesing. Gustav Tafel, president of the Cincinnati Turners, and Judge Stallo, a German lawyer, negotiated with Mayors Fearns of Newport and Foley of Covington to have seven Turners arrested and delivered to the Covington Jail. Permission was given to the Turner women and children to cross into Cincinnati for safety.

The remaining members of the Turner group marched from the Newport ferry to the Newport Turnhall to defend themselves. A group of civilian cannoneers charged with defending against the Turners abandoned their guns when they saw the approaching Turner group, and the Turner sharpshooter Carl Spinner (nicknamed "Zwirbelschuetze," or Twirl Shooter), who had been arrested, was abandoned by the sheriff, who ran to safety from the approaching Turners. After the men secured themselves inside, the Newport Turnhall was surrounded by a mob commanded by Sheriff Striker, demanding the surrender of their arms.

The Turners smuggled their arms out and across the river to Cincinnati overnight, and then 120 Turners marched to the Covington Courthouse for a preliminary hearing conducted by two magistrates. After seven days, 31 Turners were turned over to the Kenton County, Kentucky Circuit Court on felony charges of attempted murder, with bond of several thousand dollars apiece. After a two-year trial defended by Cincinnati German judge Stallo and Kentucky lawyer Stevenson, all defendants were declared not guilty and discharged. Several wealthy Kentucky Germans put up the bond for all the Turners arrested and held—totaling $80,000.[46]

Haunted by the fear of this mob violence and persecution at the hand of the Know-Nothings, some Cincinnati and northern Kentucky Turners decided to form settlement societies, or "Little Germanies," to establish their own German communities away from the areas of nativist concentration.

The first of these settlements was New Ulm, Minnesota. On March 29, 1855, Cincinnati and Newport Turner cofounder Wilhelm Pfaender wrote an article called "Practical Turnerism" in the *Turnzeitung*, the Turner newspaper, suggesting that the Turners form one of the Little Germanies "in a neighborhood in the west to be determined later, in proportion to available capital, to acquire a stretch of land of which part would be laid out as a city, the remainder partly as a reserve, and partly as farmland for those to be determined, who prefer agricultural operations to ownership in the city." Pfaender called for the formation of a settlement society as a stock venture, with each stockholder being entitled to lots and lands in accordance with the investment.

Pfaender was in luck. In 1854, a Chicago Landverein had been set up, made up of members of the Chicago Turnverein who had the same idea as Pfaender to form a sheltered all-German community. The National Turnerbund, or Federation of Turners, gave Cincinnati Turners the authority to lead this project. Cincinnati sent a delegation of three Turners from the Turner Colonization Society of Cincinnati in late 1855 to visit New Ulm: Wilhelm Pfaender, Wilhelm Seeger and mineralogist Leo Los. The three were so impressed by their warm reception at New Ulm that they decided to buy land from the first settlers of the Chicago Landverein under some conditions. The Chicago company sold six construction sites and some others in four-acre lots around the town for thirty-three dollars in cash to each of its two hundred members.[47]

In 1857, seventy German families, totaling nearly 1,300 people, most of them Cincinnati and Newport Turners, boarded the steamship *Frank Steele* in Cincinnati. It took them westward down the Ohio River to the Mississippi River, where it then headed north to Minnesota. The steamer arrived in New Ulm on May 7, 1857, after an entire month-long trip because the Mississippi River froze over at Lake Pepin. The Chicago and Cincinnati/Newport Turner groups merged, and New Ulm was incorporated by an act of the Minnesota state legislature in 1857. In 1857, Wilhelm Pfaender helped to form his third Turner Society, the New Ulm Turnverein.

For the founders of New Ulm, Minnesota, starting this new German town was like jumping out of the frying pan and into the fire. In 1862, only a few years after their arrival, New Ulm was attacked by the native Sioux Indians, resulting in large devastation of the settlement and loss of lives. But New Ulm rebuilt and continued to prosper as a German community. The Turners in Cincinnati sent their friends a Howitzer cannon from Cincinnati to New Ulm to help their brothers ward off the attack of the Sioux Indians.

Another example of these "Little Germanies" was the town of Egg Harbor, New Jersey. One Cincinnati Turner, Johann Heinrich Henke, owned lots in Egg Harbor that passed to his great-grandsons, who donated the land for park use to the State of New Jersey in the 1990s. The settlement was established in 1854 with the building of the Camden and Atlantic Railroad, which connected the big East Coast lines running through Philadelphia, Pennsylvania, and the newly opened seaside resort of Atlantic City. A land association was formed, selling shares for $300, and the town was incorporated on March 16, 1858.

The association invested a sizeable amount of money in a large national marketing campaign to settle Egg Harbor. These advertising campaigns were targeted at German Americans or newly arrived immigrants from German-speaking countries. Advertisements in the *Baltimore Correspondent* in 1858 mention regular Egg Harbor sales agents in Philadelphia, New York, Boston, Newark, Buffalo, Cleveland, Baltimore and Washington. Only two years later, the association had agents in twenty-nine cities of the United States as far west as St. Louis and Milwaukee.

Fifteen years after its settlement, Egg Harbor was a nationally advertised German American undertaking, an experiment that Germans all over the country watched with great interest. Most German American newspapers in about 1860 provided regular progress reports on the growth of the colony. Advertisements in the German Cincinnati papers in 1860 made the reader believe that if he invested $500 in Egg Harbor, his children and even grandchildren would have no worries whatsoever. There was even enough support in the early years for two Turner Societies—the Vorwaerts and Germania Turnvereine of Egg Harbor. The hope of the developers of Egg Harbor came to fruition: Egg Harbor became an exclusively German community and stayed so for more than half a century.[48]

By 1875, the Cincinnati Turners had 340 members who were gymnasts, divided into three divisions: 50 members over eighteen, 70 members between fourteen and eighteen and 220 children below fourteen.[49] The second floor of the Turnhall housed the German theater, which remained until World War I, with a capacity of 18,000 people, performing shows Friday and Sunday evenings from late fall to early spring. Cincinnati Germans in the Turner theater's heyday could see theater in their mother tongue, with such titles as *Herz und Dollar.* The third floor housed a concert room and also business rooms for Turner Society directors. The organization had a sixty-member Turner cadet corps, an eighteen-piece Turner band and a twenty-five-voice singing choir.

In that same year, 1875, a history of the original founders of the Cincinnati Turners was published, a sort of "Where Are They Now?" article. The article demonstrated the respect that Cincinnati Turners reserved for their founders, some of whom had already gone to "the evergreen *Hasenheide* of mortal memory."

Carl Leopold Fettweis had a successful monument and sculpture business in Cincinnati, supplying architectural sculpture, public art and funeral monuments. Fettweis fostered artistic lives for his four sons: Leopold, Charles Jr., Hugo and Otto. Leopold Fettweis, born the year the Cincinnati Turnverein was founded, was the most successful of the sons. He sculpted the Germania statue and Apollo frieze on the German Mutual Insurance Building, the Hecker and McCook monuments in Washington Park, the Jahn Memorial in Imwood Park, the Ninth Ohio Monument in Chickamauga, Tennessee, and numerous funeral monuments in Spring Grove Cemetery. He studied in Rome in 1875 and gave instruction in clay modeling at the Ohio Mechanics Institute in 1876. Otto Fettweis was a marble cutter at his father's business. Hugo Fettweis was a lithographer in Cincinnati. Finally, Charles Jr. studied in Rome and taught sculpture at the Ohio Mechanics Institute while working for his father's business.[50]

These are a few of the fourteen founders of the Cincinnati Turnvereine in 1848. *Top row, left to right*: Rudolph Tafel, Hugo Tafel, Albert Tafel and Wilhelm Pfaender. In the center is Gustav Tafel. *Bottom row, left to right*: Hugo Gollmer, Adolph Krebs, Ferdinand Hoffmeister and Franz Hellfereich. Although Hellfereich is not listed in the records as a founder, he donated the land for the first turnplatz in 1848.

Ferdinand Hoffmeister (1827–1906) ran a men's clothing accessories store on West Seventh Street from 1842 until he passed it on to his son, Albert, in 1887. He also fought in the Civil War. He married Rosalia Klein (1826–1897), and together they had five children. His daughter, Louise (1851–1938), married another prominent Cincinnati Turner and publisher, Max Burgheim.[51]

William Pfaender moved to Newport, Kentucky, founded the Newport Turner Society in 1852 and then moved with the group of Cincinnati Turners to the Turner settlement of New Ulm, Minnesota, where he founded the New Ulm Turners. He also served in the Union army during the Civil War and was mayor of the city.

Hugo Gollmer (1830–1889) was born in Württemberg. He married Anna, born in Newport, Kentucky, and they moved (along with his mother, Catherine) to St. Louis, Missouri. He served as president, secretary and even librarian of the St. Louis Turners. He fought for the Union in the Third

This is an advertisement for Cincinnati Turner cofounder Carl Leopold Fettweis's stone monument business.

Missouri Infantry and then operated a lithography business for many years. He also became corresponding secretary for the North American Turner Union for many years, printing the yearly Turner membership reports.[52]

J.C. Eiselein was a painter in Cincinnati and died in 1849 (less than a year after the founding of the society) during the fierce cholera epidemic that also took the life of Paul Authenreith, the two-year-old brother of first-year Turners Gustav, Louis and Adolph Authenreith.

Carl Sprandel (1820–1892) was a bookkeeper and moved away from Cincinnati for a short time but then returned to work at Linz's box factory. He married and had several children. His burial record at the Walnut Hills German Protestant Cemetery lists the lot owner as "Fecht verein der turngemiende," or the Fencing Club of the Turners.[53]

Adolph Krebs (1831–1884) was born in the Bovenden bei Gottingen, near Hanover, Germany, and immigrated to Cincinnati in 1847 with his father. He apprenticed at Rowse & Scherer Lithography and afterward worked for lithographers Klauprecht and Menzel in the 1850s. He moved to Pittsburgh, Pennsylvania, living there from 1852 to 1869. There he married Fredaricka Straub (1834–1894), daughter of the owner of the Straub Brewery in Allegheny City, Pennsylvania. Returning to Cincinnati in 1869, he worked for Ehrgott & Forbriger Lithographers, the printers of the Turner lithographs, after the death of Adolph Forbriger. In 1874, Peter Ehrgott retired, and Krebs took over the company. The Krebs Lithography Company was very successful until 1888 with the help of Adolph's son, Herman Krebs. The lithographs produced at Krebs employed complex and vivid coloration, elements borrowed from classical and fine art and from adverting and promotional design of the late nineteenth century. Adolph and his wife lived in Cincinnati's Avondale neighborhood and had seven children who survived to adulthood. He became a founding and prominent member of the North Cincinnati Turners.[54]

Otto Krebs was Adolph's younger brother. In the spring of 1852, Adolph went to Pittsburgh to work for a branch of Klauprecht and Menzel Lithographers. But in the summer of 1855, Otto and Adolph opened their own lithographic firm, which Otto's brother took over and ran when Adolph returned to Cincinnati in 1869.

Gottlieb Wiest migrated from Cincinnati to Guttenberg, Iowa, and lived out his days there. Guttenberg had been founded as another German community, aided by the Western Settlement Society of Cincinnati, a semicharitable group founded to help German immigrants who wanted to settle in the American Midwest, away from anti-immigrant sentiment.[55]

The five Tafel brothers dispersed after helping to found the Cincinnati Turnverein. Richard Tafel (1835–1849) died first. Albert Tafel (1829–1868) became a pharmacist, was the American Turner Association national president from 1856 to 1858 and died in Nice, France, after trying to recover from an illness in Italy. Rudolph Tafel (1831–1893) died in London, England, where he was a Swedenborgian minister and wrote the foremost encyclopedic work on Emanuel Swedenborg, still used by the church. After completing schooling, he formed a pharmaceutical partnership but turned business over to his brother, Albert, to pursue academic life. At the age of thirty-one, he became chair of the Department of Modern Languages and Comparative Philology at Washington University in St. Louis, Missouri.[56] Hugo Tafel (1834–1862) founded the Leavenworth, Kansas Turners with nine others in July 1857.[57] Leavenworth was a strategic location on the Missouri River, at the terminus of the Santa Fe and Oregon Trails. Hugo left Leavenworth to join the Ninth Ohio Regiment with his brother Gustav but was killed at the Battle of Mill Springs. Gustav Tafel (1830–1908), the most prominent of the five Tafel brothers, went on to become founder and president of the North Cincinnati Turners and mayor of Cincinnati. In 1867, while he was an Ohio Assembly member, he helped to re-found the Columbus Turners, who had disbanded after their nativist attacks in 1855.[58]

Adhering to the social justice legacy of the Tafel family, Rich Tafel, the great-great-nephew of Gustav Tafel and founding executive director of the Log Cabin Republicans, brought the Log Cabin convention to Cincinnati, Ohio, in 1995 in protest of the 1993 passing of the discriminatory Article 12 in Cincinnati. This event set in motion its eventual overturn in 2006.

Franz Hellferich (1816–1864), who donated his empty lot to the Turners in 1848, continued to prosper in the woodturning business. Hellferich was born in Speir, Rheinpfalz, and immigrated with his wife, Sybilla, to New Orleans, Louisiana, in 1840, landing in Cincinnati in 1841. In 1854, he opened up a gristmill opposite the Turnhall on Jackson Street. He then decided to move to an area about eight miles from Cincinnati, near California, Ohio, and founded the German enclave known as Sweet Wine. This area was in the fertile Five Mile Creek Valley and was inhabited by other Rheinpfalz immigrant winemakers, some of whom supplied the wine house of Nicholas Longworth to produce his Sparkling Catawba Wine. Hellferich became first postmaster and mayor of Sweet Wine, grew grapes, produced wine and operated a tavern there near today's A.J.'s Roadhouse on Kellogg Avenue. He shortly returned to Cincinnati, where he opened another tavern and coffeehouse called the Senate Exchange on Main Street near the courthouse. In 1864, he opened up a store that sold European wines, cognac and whiskey with his three sons: Franz Jr., Charles and August. One of his grandsons, Jacques Hellferich, would be an active member of the North Cincinnati Turners in Corryville.[59]

The influence of the Cincinnati Turners is seen in their spreading of the Turner philosophy to new regions as their lives took them to other parts of the city or the country. William Pfaender, an original founder of the Central Turners, went on to found the Newport, Kentucky Turners and the New Ulm, Minnesota Turners. An interesting musical connection to William Pfaender is that Victoria Beckham, also known as Posh Spice, is his fifth great-niece through his brother, Carl Pfaender, who had been a close friend of socialists Karl Marx and Friedrich Engels in London, England.[60]

Oscar Sputh, the Turner instructor for both the Cumminsville Turners and North Cincinnati Turners in the 1880s, also served as Turner instructor for Indianapolis Turners and later the Chicago, Illinois Turners. His brother, Christian Sputh, was a prominent and active member of the Dayton, Ohio Turners, and his son, Carl Sputh Sr., was a longtime president of the Turner Normal College, now a part of Indiana University's College of Physical Education and Tourism, and also a longtime president of the Indianapolis Turnverein.

August Hoffmeister, a first-year member of the Cincinnati Turnverein and a former Turner in Germany, visited Indianapolis in 1851 and founded the Indianapolis, Indiana Turners with five other Indianapolis German immigrants: Alex and Jacob Metzger, John Ott, Karl Hill and Clemens Vonnegut (the grandfather of American pop-novelist Kurt Vonnegut).

Joe Eiselein, son of one of the Central Turner founders, was one of the original founders in 1870 of the Cumminsville Turners. Robert C.

Georgi—an early member of the Dayton, Ohio Turners and a prominent member of the Central Turners—helped to found Cincinnati's West End Turners in 1881. Gustav Tafel went on to help re-form the Columbus, Ohio Turners in 1867 after they had disbanded in the 1850s due to anti-German bashing and later the North Cincinnati Turners in 1882. His brother, Hugo Tafel, helped to found the Leavenworth, Kansas Turners in 1857.

However, the golden age of the Cincinnati Turners would not come to pass without participation in the tragic Civil War.

Cincinnati Turnvereine during the Civil War

Fight bravely for freedom and justice!
—Ninth Ohio Regiment motto

As a border city, Cincinnati had close ties with commerce across the Ohio River in Kentucky, where business partners owned slaves. There was also a great riverboat trade between Cincinnati and New Orleans, Louisiana, and Natchez, Mississippi. Hats, farm machinery and salted pork produced in Cincinnati were transported south along the Ohio in exchange for goods, like cotton, from the South. An equal amount of Confederate activity as abolitionist activity occurred in Cincinnati. Confederate bombs were alleged to have been manufactured in Cincinnati and shipped for use in combat in the South.

Before the Civil War, Cincinnati was the scene of four prosecutions against abolitionists who defied the Fugitive Slave Act. The case of William M. Connelly in 1858 attracted the most media attention. After two fugitive slaves were found in a room he had rented, an arrest resulted in several deputies being seriously injured. Connelly was defended by Turner friend Judge John B. Stallo, but he was convicted and sentenced to jail. When his brief ordeal ended, Cincinnati Turners arranged a huge celebration of his release, complete with a parade and mass meeting at which Connelly gave the major address.[61]

During the first year of the Civil War, Wendell Phillips, an abolitionist lecturer, was mobbed and attacked on March 24, 1862, at the opera house and was defended by the Cincinnati Turner guards. A song was written by Turner Wilhelm Mueller in German about the event, and it had one stanza noting that "you could hear amidst the fight and lingering gun smoke, the loud Turner cry '*Bahn Frei*' or 'Make Way,'" as the Turners led Phillips out of the opera house and to safety.[62]

The early Turners immediately adapted to their new homeland. America embodied what the early Forty-eighters immigrants wanted in the old Fatherland: fair representation in their government rather than the elitism of the royalty of the Germanic kingdoms. As the hopes of a renewed revolution in Europe fizzled in 1849, the Germans became invested in improving their new homeland. They desired to gain a voice for themselves and their culture in the America.

A year before the outbreak of the Civil War, the *Cincinnati Daily Gazette* reported how the Turners were going to celebrate July 4. The Turners celebrated the day independent of any other organization. After parading through the principal thoroughfares of the city, they would retire to Jackson Hill and spend the day after their own fashion, listening to an oration and reading the Declaration of Independence.[63]

The Cincinnati Turners' involvement in the Civil War exemplified their patriotism. Even after the previous decade of bashing by the Know-Nothing Party and Anglo-Americans, the Germans were one of the first groups in the nation to respond to President Abraham Lincoln's call for volunteers to fight for the Union. They were not the average "Billy Yank" who volunteered to fight for the Union. They were experienced German militia fighting for a German-only unit—and proud of it. Many had experience fighting in the Napoleonic wars, as well as in the campaigns of the recent 1848 revolution in Germany. Many were active members of the Turners and were more fit than their Anglo-American counterparts. Many also brought their own guns and sabers, saving the government money in arming them with military-issued weapons. This was something that the members of the Ninth Ohio would bring up repeatedly in their letters to the Cincinnati German papers—something that they felt the native Anglo-American papers didn't mention enough in reference to them.

On the evening of April 17, three days after the bombardment of Fort Sumter, a mass meeting of German Americans was held in the Turnhall on Walnut Street to plan for the formation of an exclusively German infantry regiment. The leader of this formation was Robert L. McCook, the Scotch-Irish law partner of Judge John B. Stallo, a man who had defended the Turners in the Pentecost Monday Riots in Covington, Kentucky, in the

1850s. The Turnhall was overflowing with men, and in short order, the plan to form a German regiment was enthusiastically adopted. Gustav Tafel said that news of the outbreak of the Civil War on April 26, 1861, in Cincinnati "caused an uproar beyond description. The Turnhall on Walnut Street, hummed like a beehive," and when Tafel proposed enlistment, the rolls "filled with the men eager to fight against slavocracy."[64] In less than twenty-four hours, the muster roll of the regiment had been signed by 500 men in excess of the 1,014 who could be accepted; 300 members of the regiment were Turners, and of the 1,135 officers and men in the regiment, all but McCook himself were German.

The Cincinnati Turners exclusively formed four of the ten companies of the Ninth. The other units may have had Cincinnati Turners but were not exclusively Turner members, even though they were exclusively German. Company A was raised by committee at the Cincinnati Turnhall and was composed of Cincinnati and Newport Turners. Company B was composed of Cincinnati and Hamilton Turners, and Companies C and D were formed of Cincinnati Turners. August Willich recruited companies E through H

This is a recruiting advertisement that ran in the *Cincinnati Volksfreund* on February 15, 1862, after the Ninth Ohio had been formed.

All the Cincinnati Turners who served in the Ninth Ohio under Gustav Kaemmerling. The founder of the Cumminsville Turners, Wilhelm Sanders, is in the upper left corner. *Courtesy of Cincinnati Central Turners.*

of the Ninth at Arbeitershalle (Workingman's Hall) in Over-the-Rhine, and two preexisting German militia units, the Jaegers and the Lafayette Militia, formed Companies J and K, respectively.[65] There was also at least one Dayton Turner, Gustav Bergmann, a teacher from Prussia who had joined the Dayton Turner Society in 1856. Bergmann was credited as being the first American teacher to enlist in the Civil War. His son, Erick Bergmann, would become the Turner instructor for the Cumminsville Turners in 1894. There were also at least two Lexington, Kentucky Turners, who joined after proving their athletic ability by jumping a fence.

The regiment was formed as the Ninth Ohio Volunteer Infantry, but to its family and friends in the Cincinnati German community, they were known as "Die Neuner." The Germans of the Ninth Ohio were resentful of being scorned by Anglo-American nativists in their own Union army, who called them "Dutchmen," "Damn Dutch," "sauerkrauts" and even worse names. Their Rebel counterparts nicknamed them "Dutch Devils," "Bully Dutchmen," "Bloody Dutch" and "German Mercenaries" because of their vigorous fighting and infamous bayonet charges.[66]

The drillmaster of the regiment was General August von Willich. A drill area was immediately established on the Orphan Grounds at Fourteenth and Elm, where Music Hall now stands. The regiment quickly learned the Prussian system of drill, with which Von Willich was very familiar. The unit members also took their commands in the field in German throughout their campaign.[67]

Within three days of its formation, Die Neuner had its first parade, led by the twenty-five-member Turner Band under the leadership of Guenther Siedensticker (1836–1887), and on April 24, the regiment marched to Camp Harrison, formed on the trotting park between Spring Grove Cemetery and Carthage on the outskirts of Cumminsville. There the men set up a shantytown of frame shacks until tents could be procured. Narrow streets between the rows of shanties were named Main, Walnut and Race, as well as after other streets in their Over-the-Rhine neighborhood, and boasted edifices such as a Turnhall, Deutsche Republik, Arbeitershalle and Saengerhalle. The English-speaking regiments proudly displayed the names of their Cincinnati institutions, like Pike's Opera House and the Burnett House.[68]

The Ninth participated in several actions and skirmishes: the Battle of Rich Mountain, West Virginia (July 10, 1861); Carnifex ferry, West Virginia (September 10, 1861); the Battle of Mill Springs, Kentucky (January 19, 1862); operations against Corinth, Mississippi; the Battle of Perryville, Kentucky (October 8, 1862); Hoover's Gap, Tennessee (June 26, 1863); the Tullahoma campaign; the Battle of Chickamauga, Georgia (September 19 and 20, 1863); the Battle of Missionary Ridge near Chattanooga, Tennessee (November 25, 1863); and, in the early part of the 1864 Atlanta Campaign, at Buzzard Roost, Georgia (February 25, 1862), and in the Battle of Resaca, Georgia.[69]

Two histories were written about the Ninth in German. The first, *We Were the Ninth*, was written in 1897 by Constantin Grebner. Although he was not a member of the Ninth, he interviewed former regimental members and their families and read their letters and diaries. Gustav Tafel wrote a 1901 history about Ohio Germans in the Civil War, including the Ninth. Because both of these histories were written nearly forty years after the end of the Civil War, they seem to be glorified, and even "enhanced," memories rather than contemporary diaries.

The most authentic history of the Ninth Ohio comes from the letters of Lieutenant Friedrich Bertsch and Chaplain Wilhelm Stangel. The ninety-eight letters of Bertsch were written between June 1, 1861, and September

11, 1862, to the *Cincinnati Volksfreund*; Stangel's ten letters were published in the *Louisville Anzeiger* between August 11, 1861, and August 26, 1862. Their correspondence provides an intimate portrait of the German Americans fighting in the Union, a perspective all but absent from the Anglo-American press of the time. Both men talk of the regiment's displeasure with not being paid for many months, the lack of military training or strategy from the Anglo-American generals and volunteers, the lack of good camp food, the rare pleasure of lager beer and the continued anti-German sentiment that they faced.

The Turners from Hamilton, Ohio, who made up a portion of Company B, were led by Hamilton Turnverein physical instructor William Margedant. Like Cincinnati, Hamilton had many early German immigrants, whose influence showed in culture, architecture and food. The paper industry, ironworks, malting/brewing and manufacturing works thrived in Hamilton in the early to mid-twentieth century due to the skill of German immigrant workers.

William C. Margedant (1835–1900) was born in Dusseldorf, Germany, and arrived in Hamilton, Ohio, in 1855 to escape being part of the king's royal guard. He owned a woodworking machinery company, and he was the author of fourteen U.S. patents. In 1861, he was the physical instructor for the Hamilton Turnverein, and upon hearing President Abraham Lincoln's call for volunteers, he went to the various German-owned shops in Hamilton and rounded up his Turners to join the Ninth Ohio Regiment forming in Cincinnati. He became known for his pioneering mapmaking skills, using early photographic methods to reproduce quickly—this gave him the title "Pathfinder of the Army of the Cumberland." He left the Ninth Ohio after only three months to serve Generals William Rosencrans, John Freemont and Turner Franz Siegel.[70]

The names of Margedant's Turner volunteers from Hamilton who joined the Ninth Regiment are engraved today on Hamilton's Soldiers Monument:

> *Wm Margedant, Captain, Theodore Racek 2nd Lt, Caspar Decher, sergeant, John Schmidt Corporal, Phillip Menninger, Wagoner, Clement Breitenback, Lewis Blatterman Michael Brooker* [Brucker], *Henry Jend, Robert Kaulig, George Lanber, Julius Lessing, Adam Laufer, John Orion, Eduard Scheurer, Jacob Schlosser, and the musicians—Daniel Sallee, George Leveline, Henry Tepart, John H. Garver, Ernst Miller, Joseph Kililan, John Kuehnle, and George Schweinfest.*

A uniformed William C. Margedant, physical instructor for the Hamilton Turnverein and the musterer of Hamilton Turners for the Ninth Ohio Regiment.

The Newport Turners who joined the ranks of the Ninth were led by Sergeant Herman Ponitz, former administrator of the Turnhall in Newport. He was promoted to second lieutenant in Company A in August 1862, while the regiment was in Alabama, after a number of officers had resigned due to illnesses. Ponitz would replace Gustav Tafel after he left the 9th to form the 106th Regiment.[71] Other Ohio regiments that were composed of Turners were the 28th, 37th, 106th and 108th Regiments.

The Ninth officially mustered in as a three-month regiment at a horse trotting park called Camp Harrison, located between Cumminsville and Carthage, Ohio, on May 8, 1861. Ten days later, the men marched to Camp Dennison, about two miles north of Milford, Ohio. They were then mustered for three years on May 27, 1861.[72]

While at Camp Dennison, the Ninth received its regimental colors, consisting of thirteen gold stars on a field of blue silk above a pennant. Inscribed on the flag were the words "Zu Cincinnatis erste deutsche Riege" ("To Cincinnati's First German Regiment"), and on the front was the regiment's motto, "Kampfet brav fur Freiheit und Recht" ("Fight Bravely for Freedom and Justice"). Elise Arnold and Karoline Gresin made the flag, and Dr. Bauer presented the colors to McCook at camp on May 10, 1861. Sergeant Phillip Fitz of Company I was named standard-bearer for the regiment.[73]

The first battle in which the Ninth distinguished itself was in the January 19, 1862 battle at Mill Springs, Kentucky, about 130 miles southeast of Louisville, near the current town of Nancy, Kentucky. Also known by the Union as the Battle of Logan's Cross Roads and by the Confederacy as the Battle of Fishing Creek, the Ninth performed the first bayonet charge of the Civil War to help defeat the Confederates. It concluded an early Confederate offensive in Kentucky, and although considered a small battle in comparison to others, it was the second largest in Kentucky. Eight hundred Confederate and two hundred Union soldiers were killed and wounded at the battle.[74] It was the first significant Union victory in the war and was much celebrated in the popular press. Confederate general Felix Zollicoffer, considered the mastermind of the Confederacy and someone with great potential, was slain by a member of the Fourth Kentucky Regiment in this battle.[75]

Corporal Hugo Tafel, one of the young founders of the Cincinnati Turnverein and brother of Gustav Tafel, was mortally wounded at the battle and died shortly thereafter. Friedrich Bertsch immortalized Hugo's last minutes in a letter written to and published in the *Cincinnati Volksfreund* on January 25, 1862:

> *He gave our chaplain Fuchsburger a handshake and last greetings to his comrades, his parents, and brother, and to his beloved wife, as they, his victorious comrades, came through the night camp. How often he delighted his friends in Cincinnati, and in the camp with his pretty songs, always lively and cheerful, and now the singer has been put out of tune and the wreath of victory lays around his pale head on Kentucky's bloody ground. May his brave conduct and his noble soldier's death console his friends and beloved relatives over his painful wound and the never withering evergreen planted over his gravesite be a respectful remembrance.*[76]

In all, six members of the Ninth perished at the Battle of Mill Springs.

This Currier and Ives lithograph shows the Ninth Ohio in a bayonet charge at the Battle of Mill Springs. *Courtesy of Kentucky Historical Society.*

One month after the battle, General McCook received the remnants of the regiment's flag from the battle in an envelope that also contained a letter from Nanette B. Smith, president of the Royal Ladies Society of Louisville: "As a testimonial to our appreciation of the gallant conduct of your regiment in the battle of Mill Springs, Jan. 19., I transmit with this note a flag to be presented in the name of the Royal Ladies of Louisville…I cannot express the grateful feelings of our hearts in appropriate words, but must cordially thank the officers and men under your command."

The note and flag remnants hang preserved in a glass frame at Memorial Hall in Cincinnati's Over-the-Rhine, across from the McCook Monument at Washington Park.

The Ninth at the Battle of Mill Springs captured the flag of the Nineteenth Tennessee Volunteer Infantry, Company D, known as the Gillespie Guards. Proud of their victory and their spoils, the Turners of the Ninth sent the flag and other booty[77] back to the Turnhall on Walnut Street for display, according to a February 1862 *Louisville Journal* article. A plea was made by the Tennessee State Museum in Nashville in October 2009 for Cincinnati to return the missing flag, which has yet to be found.[78]

The Ninth would be well known for its fierce bayonet charges throughout its three-year service in the Civil War. The sound of a chorus of loud, spirited German hurrahs must have struck terror in the hearts of the Confederates, as they knew that they would soon be looking point-down into a sea of bayonets. One Turner manufacturer of these bayonets was Rudolph Hug, listed as a cutler and maker of dental instruments in Cincinnati in the 1850s. Nine of these original Hug-marked Turner bayonets (called Yatagan blades) made in Cincinnati are known to exist in the hands of avid Civil War collectors. They were massive knives, measuring 18.0 inches long by 1.5 inches wide, and had engraved on the hilt the German phrase "Bahn Frei," which means "Make Way."[79]

On March 24, 1862, the day of the Schleswig-Holstein uprising against the Germanic monarchy in 1848 was celebrated in small circles by the Schleswig-Holstein immigrants in the Ninth while in Spring Hill, Tennessee. Captain Ferdinand Mueller (a Cincinnati Turner) from the Second Company, Captain Schroeder of the Fourth Company and Captain Thoensen of the Seventh Company had stood in the ranks of the Schleswig-Holstein army at that time.[80] These veterans of the wars in Europe pointed out that riding, driving and marching were harder in America than on the well-maintained roads of Europe. European soldiers were typically quartered with civilian families in proportions appropriate to the size of the house, rather than fending for themselves like in America. This, they claimed, formed affiliations that prevented the brutality seen during the Civil War on both sides.[81]

The Ninth's band became famous as it proceeded with the unit through its campaigns, entertaining Union supporters and German immigrants and maintaining the regimental morale. While the regiment was near Buchanan, Virginia, in July 1861, it entertained fellow civilian immigrants:

> *We had much amusement however in that an old German married couple who had immigrated here from Donaushingen in Baden about 20 years ago and who lived about 10 miles from here, danced a waltz with great precision, according to older fashion to the sounds of our band on the grass in our camp. The wife, a sprightly matron about seventy years old, and the man was about the same and just as cheerful and lively. They had not heard music and been regaled by German music tunes in many years and enjoyed themselves heartily among their native landsmen.*[82]

While moving through Virginia, the civilian reaction to hearing the Ninth Ohio regimental band play was recorded by Friedrich Bertsch:

> *Our regiment's band…caused a sensation everywhere they played and has a nice selection of pieces. When the music sounded today in our new camp it was surrounded by all the residents in the neighborhood and listened to with the greatest pleasure. On this occasion there were people located among the crowd, who never before heard a music band. This discovery amused us Cincinnatians accustomed to music to the largest degree.*[83]

After a twenty-mile march to Huttonsville, West Virginia, in August 1861, Friedrich Bertsch reported, "While the music played we no longer felt weariness."[84]

Albin Stecher joined the Ninth in August 1861 in Camp New Creek Station, Virginia, as musician first class in the regimental band. After the war, he became fitness instructor for the Cincinnati Turners.[85] He was also the last surviving member of the Ninth Ohio Regiment.

While in its first campaign in Camp New Creek Station, the Ninth Ohio held a camp celebration on August 17, 1861, in honor of the German Turnfest being held in Berlin, Germany, where a memorial dedicated to Friedrich Ludwig Jahn, the Turner founder, was to be dedicated. The men celebrated through music and song and heard an address by Gustav Tafel on the importance of the event in Berlin: "A drinking horn made in camp and filled with beer rotated around here several times; many cheers emerged about Germany's and America's unity and a lot of wishful thinking was enthusiastically expressed."[86]

The Ninth's Turners would practice gymnastics in the field when they could between campaigns. While in Nashville, Tennessee, in 1862, they used cannonballs for "so-called nature gymnastics, shot put, throwing high and wide, and built a swing, built from splendid wild vines hanging from trees."[87]

The ladies of Cumberland wanted to entertain the officers of the Ninth with dinner in the camp. A Turnfest was planned for Sunday, August 17, so that the regiment could impress the ladies with their gymnastic and athletic abilities. The men prepared by taking baths, combing and brushing their hair and beards and polishing their uniforms. In addition to a festive meal, drinking, the customary speech, music, song, gymnastics, fencing and dancing were also planned. The German beer brewers of Cumberland even graciously sent thirty-eight barrels of beer as a gift. However, a call to the next battle prevented this event from happening.[88]

The two-day battle of Chickamauga was the bloodiest in which the Ninth fought. About 51 percent of the regiment perished in the battle. The men gallantly defended the Union and again received accolades for their courage in the field. The first day, they were tasked with guarding the trains, but when they saw that the fighting was furious, the Ninth swept far beyond the Union front without waiting for orders, charged two Confederate brigades and regained the Union battery that they had taken. The morning of the second day, the Ninth charged with Van Derveer's brigade across Kelly Field full into the face of Breckinridge's advancing division. It pushed on to the cannon that had been supporting the Confederate advance, disabling the whole battery. Finally in the afternoon came the real fervor for the Ninth at Chickamauga. The men charged into position on Snodgrass Hill and cleared the slopes in front of it with bayonets three times in succession.[89]

Reverend Carl Tuerk, pastor of the German Evangelical Church on the west side of Walnut between Eighth and Ninth Streets, wrote a poem about Chickamauga immortalizing the bravery of the Ninth. One excerpt seems to capture the anxiety and commitment of the unit before the bayonet charge: "Brother, speak to my wife if I fall, tell my child, and give my regards to my loved ones all. Kiss me yourself, Brother one last time!"[90]

On December 30, 1863, the Ninth was in Chattanooga, Tennessee, when its three-year term of service was nearly up. The men were asked to

This is a depiction of the Ninth Ohio leading another bayonet charge against the Confederate army at the Battle of Chickamauga on Snodgrass Hill, near where its monument stands today. *Courtesy of Chickamauga and Chattanooga National Military Park.*

reenlist, but after brief discussion, they decided that they had seen enough and chose not to reenlist as some of their other brother regiments did. This, of course, received great criticism from nativists in the Cincinnati Anglo-American press despite the men's valiant defense of the Union in their many campaigns.

At 8:00 a.m. on Friday, May 24, 1864, friends and relatives of the Ninth Ohio, and other Turners with the Turner Music Corps, reached the Ohio River wharf in Cincinnati to meet the sunburned and fatigued men of the Ninth returning home by steamboat. After joyous and tearful reunions, they marched en masse back to Turnhall for a homecoming celebration amid singing, dancing and revelry that lasted far into the night.

The Ninth Ohio was summoned to Turnhall on June 2, 1864, and officially mustered out by Colonel Gustav Kaemmerling. Back pay for the men's service, along with the promised $100 bounty for staying the full three years, was paid out to their satisfaction. Then, on June 11, a banquet at Turnhall was planned in their honor, prepared by the Cincinnati, Covington and Newport Ladies' Auxiliaries. Just as he had addressed them in Turnhall when they left, Judge Stallo addressed the Turners at the banquet and cheered them back into peaceful civilian life.[91]

On January 14, 1870, former members of the Ninth who lived in Cincinnati formed the Associated Veterans of the Ninth Regiment, Ohio Volunteer Infantry. August Witte was elected president, Friedrich Bertsch secretary and Heinrich Gunklack treasurer. In 1897, there were 125 members who met monthly at the Central Turnhall. A constitution was adopted that called for annual commemorations of the Battle of Mill Springs (January 19), the day of mustering in the regiment (May 27), the death of Colonel McCook (August 6) and the Battle of Chickamauga (September 19).[92]

Three of these posts in Cincinnati were associated with the Ninth Ohio Regiment: the Hecker Post No. 638, the August Willich Post No. 195 and the Robert L. McCook Post No. 30 in Carthage. The Israel Ludlow Post No. 76 in Cumminsville, founded on May 19, 1881, was named after Israel Ludlow, the founder of Cumminsville, but had members who had fought in other German units and who later became Cumminsville Turners. National and Ohio membership in the Grand Army of the Republic (GAR) peaked in 1890 at about 409,000 and 49,011 members, respectively. Cincinnati in 1898 hosted the GAR National Encampment.[93]

Two veteran units, the 28th Ohio Volunteer Infantry Association and Hecker Post No. 638, met monthly at Central Turnhall. The 106th Ohio Volunteer Infantry Association was led by Gustav Tafel and Frank Werner and was also made up of Cincinnati and Newport Turners. The 108th Ohio Volunteer Infantry Association was made up of Turners from Cincinnati and Covington, as well as one man who, for a brief time, had been a member of the Lick Run Turners.[94]

In 1875, Fredrick J. Werner (1830–1911), a Forty-eighter Cincinnati Turner, donated a marble memorial to those Cincinnati Turners who had perished in the Civil War. The monument is a carved six-foot-high column topped with a Spartan helmet lying over a laurel wreath.[95] Engraved on the column in gold are the names of 20 Cincinnati Turners who perished: F. Bortz, A Beyland, Wm. Dreve, Ph. Fueller, G. Hartner, F. Ludwig, H. Reintanz, H. Tafel, F. Voll, L. Frohmann, S. Biery, Wm. Belsit, H. Elzner, F. Hildenbrand, G. Kiefer, F. Mueller, F. Sattler, G. Vonau, J. Weiss and H.O. Schnetzer. The monument originally stood in a small hallway in the Walnut Street Turnhall but was moved to Memorial Hall in 1972. Now it is displayed on the second-floor gallery of Memorial Hall next to Music Hall. Other Turner Societies reported their losses in the *Turnzeitung*:

Philadelphia lost 30 men, St. Louis lost 22, Chicago lost 24 and Milwaukee lost 27, with the New York City–area Turner Societies suffering the greatest loss at 141 members.[96]

In about 1875, former regimental bugler of the Ninth Richard Meinhardt conceived the idea of a statue to honor the regiment's esteemed general. A committee of veterans was formed to erect a monument in Washington Park to honor General Robert L. McCook. Funds of $6,000 were raised from the Turners and the Cincinnati German community, and Leopold Fettweis, son of Cincinnati Turner founder C.L. Fettweis, was chosen as the artist.

This is a photo of the Turner fallen soldier memorial donated by Fredrick Werner. *Courtesy of Memorial Hall.*

McCook's mother, Martha Latimer McCook, was present at the dedication ceremony on August 23, 1877, along with his sister, Mrs. Dowling, and a brother. When sculptor Fettweis asked Mrs. McCook if she thought that any changes to her son's likeness were needed, she replied, "Certainly not! The bust represents Robert as he was in life. Nothing in it can be improved!" Mrs. McCook epitomized motherly grief during the Civil War. Her husband, Daniel, and eight sons fought in the Civil War—there was scarcely a battle that took place that did not involve one of her own. Her ultimate sacrifice was the loss of her husband and three sons in the war. Mrs. McCook delighted in being called "Mother McCook" by the Ninth Ohio veterans. At the dedication ceremony, she also said to the assembled Ninth veterans, "Whenever you decorate Robert's grave, don't forget that of his mother!"[97]

The Ninth staged a celebration afterward at Fiedel Bader's popular Turner hangout, Washington Platform, located at the corner of Court and Elm Streets, with drinking to the day's speakers. Filled with liquid *gemütlichkeit*, the veteran revelers then serenaded the McCook family at the Grand Hotel.

In 1878, several members of the regiment visited the battlefield at Mill Springs via the Cincinnati Southern Railway, which went to Somerset, Kentucky, a little town eleven miles from the battlefield. Six soldiers who had

Above, left: This is the monument of General McCook in Cincinnati's Washington Park, designed by Turner sculptor Leopold Fettweis.

Above, right: This is the monument to the Ninth Ohio at the Chickamauga and Chattanooga National Military Park, designed by Leopold Fettweis.

perished at the battle, and who had been buried in Somerset, were removed and reinterred in the national cemetery established less than a mile from the battlefield after the war.[98]

Cincinnati Turner artist Leopold Fettweis Jr. was again called on to design a monument on Snodgrass Hill at the Chickamauga and Chattanooga National Military Park in Oglethorpe, Georgia, to commemorate the victory of the Ninth Ohio in that battle. The memorial was dedicated on September 18, 1895.[99] A bronze frieze sits on a trapezoidal granite base, with a small bronze medallion and upturned acorn, the emblem of the Fourteenth Army Corps (to which the Ninth belonged in that battle). The frieze depicts a bearded member of the Ninth Ohio, perhaps flag-bearer Phillip Fitz, holding the regimental flag in his right hand, with his rifle in his left.

In 1897, Friedrich Bertsch epitomized the feeling of the Turner veterans of the Ninth:

> *Finally, let us wish that the Ninth's sons and daughters never forget what their fathers had to suffer. Meanwhile the sons and grandsons should stay*

> *fit through physical training (hiking, gymnastics, etc.). Then they can be drilled into soldiers in a month, ready not only to march and shoot but also to bear the hardships of a military campaign—hardships that demand real men. And so, in the hours of need, may sons do as fathers did, and stand up for the freedom of the Republic!*

And many Turner sons and grandsons did just that in the upcoming world wars.[100]

THE TURNERS AND THEIR TURNFESTS

Gut Heil!
—Turner greeting, meaning "Good Health!"

The Turnfest was the pinnacle event for a Turner. It was a Turner's time to show off his gymnastic and athletic prowess. Starting in the early 1850s, some Turners would travel considerable distances to compete against other Turnvereine in national, district and circuit Turnfests. Each of the three elements of Turner exercise was employed: obligatory exercise, elective sport and competitive games.

The first Turnfest in America was held September 29–30, 1851, in Philadelphia, Pennsylvania, while the first Turnfest in Germany was held in 1860 in Coburg, Germany. So the competitive Turnfest was really a German American invention.[101] These Germanic sporting events also preceded the first modern Olympics in Athens, Greece, in 1896. There were Bundesturnfests (national Turnfests) in which all the Turnvereine in the United States were invited, as well as Bezirkturnfests (local district Turnfests) that were made up of the local societies in a region. They consisted of a variety of competitions, resembling today's track and field events, with several other events added over the years. Members competed singularly in events and were awarded prizes or medals. At the end of a Turnfest, the Turnverein whose members achieved the largest number of medals was given an honor. By the start of the twentieth century, Turnfests were grand social events, with large receptions, musical and theatrical performances and parades.

The first Turnfest in Cincinnati was held from September 27 to 28, 1852, a year after the first American Turnfest. Cincinnati also hosted national Turnfests in 1855, 1865, 1873, 1889 and 1909. Cincinnati Turner teams would compete in other national Turnfests over the years. They would also compete at several German Turnfests, including 1880 in Frankfurt and 1913 in Leipzig.

The Turners were the first American cross-trainers, understanding that specializing in one activity was not good for the physical development of the entire body. At a Turner convention in Chicago, Illinois, in 1854, the National Turner Association adopted a resolution that demanded participating American Turner Societies to hold gymnastics tournaments with ten activities: horizontal bar, parallel bars, rings, pommel horse, high jump, climbing, wrestling, shot put or stone throwing, runs with and without hurdles and javelin throws. Prizes were given for other sports like fencing, shooting, swimming, skating and walking on stilts.[102]

As early as 1873, lively debates were held in the Covington Turnhall about boxing contests as part of the curriculum in the gym, and strong opposition was maintained, claiming that boxing was below the standard of physical education and should not be tolerated by Turners. Although boxing was never mandated as a nationally approved sport for Turners in Turnfests, several Cincinnati Turner Societies hosted boxing tournaments at their halls. Because of the popularity of the sport in Cincinnati and northern Kentucky, both the North Cincinnati and Newport, Kentucky Turners hosted boxing tournaments at their halls. The Covington Turners had their own boxing team in the 1910s.[103]

The events staged at a Turnfest were a cross between what we consider modern gymnastics and track and field events, with a little bit of a strongman competition thrown in: running (*laufen*), hop-skip-jump (*dreisprung*), horizontal bar (*hangeln*), stone tossing (*steinstossen*), stone lifting (*stein stemming*), high jumping (*hochspringen*), pole vaulting (*stabhochspringen*), far jumping (*weitspringen)*, rings (*ringeln*), exercises with Indian clubs (*keulenschwingen*), wrestling (*stossstechen*) and weightlifting (*gewicht stemmen*). Swimming competitions (*schwimmen*) and sharpshooting (*sharfshiesen*) were also a part of many Turnfests, like the Cincinnati Bundesturnfests of 1889 and 1909.

Women's and men's group acrobatic dancing and formation also became parts of the Turnfests in the 1910s and later, and they started to resemble more of a drill team competition. By the 1950s, focus in the Cincinnati Turnverein was less about gymnastics and more about organized sports like baseball, volleyball, basketball, bowling and golf.

The first national Turnfest in Cincinnati in 1852 was attended by Turners from Louisville, New York, Pittsburgh, Baltimore and Madison, Indiana. The competition took place at a grandstand in northern Kentucky, with an evening ball held at the Cincinnati Turnhall. The Turnfest was followed by a meeting of the Turnerbund attended by twenty-nine societies from New York, New Jersey, Ohio, Indiana, Kentucky, Pennsylvania, Missouri and Connecticut.[104]

Cincinnati also hosted the national Turnfest from September 15 to 18, 1855, where its members dominated the prize trophies. Hertel from Cincinnati won first prize in gymnastics; John L. Schreiber won first in fencing; Friedrich Bauerlein, Mr. Meier and August Eberle won in pistol shooting; Mueller and Bruckel won in rifle shooting; and Wilhelm Rothacker won the mental Turner competition.[105]

One early young star gymnast of the Cincinnati Turners was Adolph Luethy. Born in 1841 in Switzerland, he immigrated with his parents to Cincinnati in 1849. As a student of the Cincinnati Turner school, he acquired a high degree of gymnastic skill while still in his early youth. He took national first prizes at the 1858 Belleville Turnfest and the 1859 St. Louis Turnfest, becoming an active Cincinnati Turner in 1860. At the

This is a lithograph of the 1865 Turnfest in Cincinnati at Parker's Grove (which later became Coney Island) on the Ohio River, sketched by young Cincinnati artist Henry Farny. It shows the various gymnastics competitions present in Turnfests at the time.

Meyer's Swimming Hall, where local and national Turnfest swimming competitions were staged in Cincinnati. The Ohio River was also the scene of swimming competitions at the 1889 Cincinnati Turnfest.

outbreak of the Civil War, he enlisted in Company A of the Ninth Ohio Volunteer Regiment, in which he served three years before mustering out. In 1869, he moved to New York and set himself up as a jeweler.[106]

The 1865 Cincinnati National Turnfest was the first Turnfest held after the end of the Civil War. It also hosted a national meeting of physical education teachers—the first of its kind in the history of American education. The 1865 Turnfest in Cincinnati was held September 2–6 at Parker's Grove, which later became Coney Island, in Anderson Township on the Ohio River. The Pittsburgh Turnverein won the most medals of any Turner Society. A large glass trophy etched in German with the words "Den BundesTurnfest in Cincinnati 2–6 Sept 1865 gewindnet von dem Pittsburgh Turnverein" at the Cincinnati Central Turnhall memorializes their win. Other first-prize winners included Cincinnati Turners Mr. Franke (high jump), B. Froehling (weightlifting), E. Nadler (bayonet exercises), J. Baer (rifle shooting) and D. Schultz (pistol shooting).[107]

Cincinnati held its fourth national Turnfest at Imwood Park in Clifton June 26–29, 1873, in which ten societies and eighty-seven total Turners competed. The *New York Times* recorded the event on June 28: "This morning, all the Turner societies which had arrived to take part in the event, formed in procession and marched through the principal streets of the city, breaking rank at Imwood Park, where this afternoon and evening the programme of exercises will be observed in the competing for various prizes. There were thirty carriages in the procession, the first occupied by Governor Noyes, Mayor Johnson, and others." The group technical exercises in which all Turner Societies participated were led by Cincinnati Turner instructor Albin Stecher. Cincinnati Turner Friedrich Fender won first prize in the swimming competition.[108]

Left: Postcard of the official poster of the 1909 Thirtieth Cincinnati Bundesturnfest. *Courtesy of Don Prout.*

Below: The elaborate stage downtown at Government Square for the 1909 Turnfest. *Courtesy of Don Prout.*

Opposite, top: This 1909 Turnfest photo shows the Cincinnati Central Turner actives stretching. *Courtesy of Don Prout.*

Opposite, bottom: This 1909 Turnfest photo shows the mass Indian club exercises for women. *Courtesy of Don Prout.*

In order to show their prowess back in the Fatherland, Max Burgheim organized a trip of about five hundred members of the Cincinnati Turners, with one hundred accompanying ladies, to the Frankfurt, Germany Turnfest from July 24 to 29, 1880. They chartered an entire steamship, the *Silesia*, owned by the Hamburg American Line, the line that many of their families had used to immigrate to the United States.[109]

The next national Turnfest hosted in Cincinnati was in 1889. Before 1885, the competitors in national Turnfests consisted of the handpicked and

The mass exercises of the Cincinnati Turner boys' class at the 1909 Turnfest. *Courtesy of Kevin Grace.*

best members of the individual competing societies. As a result, only 200 to 300 men participated in these Turnfests. At the 1889 Cincinnati National Turnfest from June 22 to 26, a total of 1,543 Turners from ninety-six separate Turner Societies competed.[110] As a result, visiting Turners were lodged for free at the North, Central, West End and Cumminsville Turnhalls, as well as at Henry Wielert's on Vine Street. This was the first national Turnfest in which competitive gymnastics between societies was introduced, and this greatly increased the number of participants. The festival location was in the West End near the intersection of Western Avenue and Bank Street, near today's United States Post Office.

The festival opened with a grand reception for all visiting Turners at Music Hall on Saturday. The individuals and groups competed on Monday and Tuesday at the Turnfest Campus in the West End. Tuesday was the large Turner parade and picnic at Imwood Park in Clifton, sponsored by the Windisch-Mulhauser Brewery, as well as a Volksfest (cultural exhibition) at the Lookout House in Clifton. On Wednesday, there were excursions to Coney Island and the zoo.[111]

Several special sections were printed for the *Cincinnati Volksblatt* outlining the history of the local Cincinnati Turner organizations and the lineup of the grand Turnfest parade of six divisions led by the visiting

The mass exercises of the Cincinnati Turner girls' class at the 1909 Turnfest. *Courtesy of Kevin Grace.*

Turnvereine and Cincinnati veterans organizations, German choirs and German societies.

The last national Turnfest hosted in Cincinnati was the 1909 thirtieth national Turnfest, in which 1,800 Turners competed. The man responsible for making the 1909 Cincinnati Turnfest such a large undertaking was event chairman and Cincinnati Central Turner August "Garry" Hermann. He was also then president and co-owner of the Cincinnati Reds and chairman of the National Bowling Association.

The festival took place in two main locations. The Hamilton County Fairgrounds in Carthage was the Festplatz, where members set up their tents and competed in mass drills and individual competitions. The U.S. War Department loaned the Turners enough tents for two thousand participants to live, and meals were provided. The second venue was an elaborate three-block stage located on Government Square downtown and resembling a Greek temple with Corinthian columns and large allegorical statuary. The Greek discus and javelin thrower statues, which were on center stage, are now on display in the main hall at Walnut Hills High School. On the stage, Turners and other prominent athletic amateurs gave nightly exhibitions of their athletic skills. Cincinnati businessmen, realizing the importance of the revenue potential to the city, contributed $75,000 for this Turnfest.[112]

Above: This group of the Cincinnati Central Turners donning their gold lamé lederhosen costumes competed and won first prize at the Buffalo, New York Turnfest June 24–29, 1930. *Courtesy of Cincinnati German Heritage Museum.*

Below: This oddly costumed group of Cincinnati Central Turners competed at the 1936 Cleveland, Ohio National Turnfest. The *Cleveland News* headlines on July 2, 1936, read, "At Cleveland Turnfest, 5000 Watch as Cincinnati Wins." *Courtesy of Cincinnati German Heritage Museum.*

Cincinnati Central Turners who competed at the Louisville, Kentucky National Turnfest from June 15 to 20, 1921. *Courtesy of Cincinnati German Heritage Museum.*

Competing Turners registered on Wednesday, June 23, and were entertained that night by a reception at Music Hall with a mass choral exhibition by Cincinnati public schoolchildren and the United Singers of Cincinnati, with a grand ball afterward. Thursday, June 24, was the beginning of the gymnastics and field sport contests, with an allegorical and civic parade held in downtown Cincinnati, which lasted five hours and was led by Grand Marshal Julius Fleischmann, as well as a gymnastic exhibition by special classes of visiting Turners. Friday continued the gymnastics and field sport competitions, as well as mass drills by Cincinnati public schoolchildren and visiting Turners at the Cincinnati Baseball Park. Also held was an evening *Geistiges Turnfest* (Mental Turnfest) at the North Cincinnati Turnhall, consisting of singing contests, recitations and impromptu speaking. Saturday offered the mass drills of all members at the fairgrounds, the continuation of gymnastics, field sports, special contests in fencing, wrestling and swimming and exhibitions by Turners attending from Europe. That evening, a lantern parade, concert and party were also held at the fairgrounds. Sunday ended the Turnfest with the closing of contests, a Volksfest concert given by local and visiting singing societies, distribution of prizes and a grand fireworks display at Chester Park, near Cumminsville, where Gary Hermann's profile was lit in fireworks.[113] Artist Louis C. Vogt (1864–1939) memorialized one of the night performances at the Government Square stage downtown in oil.

With the ratification in 1920 of the Nineteenth Amendment giving women the right to vote, women's roles were expanding. As a result, the 1920s ushered in a new era of women's activities. The backward American Protestant view that female exercise was immoral was slowly replaced by a more liberal view of women and their roles. The American Turners supported this expanding role for women. At the Chicago Turnfest in 1921, women were allowed to compete for the first time, although they had exhibited and performed at earlier Turnfests.

The Golden Age of the Cincinnati Turners

Achieve strength through practice, enlightenment through struggle.
—early motto of the Cincinnati Turners

After the Civil War, as Turner soldiers were mustering out of service and returning home to their Turner Societies, all the Turner Societies throughout America agreed that new life needed to be breathed into the Turnerbund. Turner organizations had been decimated during the war, as their actives had left for the battlefield. This period after the Civil War led to the largest growth of the American Turner movement and to its golden age.

At a convention held at the September 1864 New York Turnfest, it was decided to retain the constitution of the old organization and give it the name Amerikansicher Turnerbund (Turner Society of America). A proclamation was issued by the central committee, calling on each individual Turner Society to organize into districts, or *turnbezirks*, and join the newly formed Turnerbund.

The American Turnerbund even changed its motto from the German Turner motto of "Frisch, Fromm, Froehlich, Frei" to "Frisch, Frei, Stark, und Treu." The American Turners organized a Normal College in New York in 1866 that is the oldest American institution for the education of teachers of physical training. Many Cincinnati Turner instructors and national society instructors graduated from this institution. The Normal College was moved to Chicago in 1871, but then the Great Chicago Fire caused it to be moved back to New York. It settled in Milwaukee, Wisconsin, from 1875 to 1888, with George Brosius as director, and from 1891 to 1907, with Brosius and George Wittich as directors. In 1907, the school was moved to Indianapolis, where it exists today as part of the college of health and tourism of Indiana State University.[114]

Cincinnati led the charge from this proclamation and formed the District Turner Union in the West on October 31, 1864, at the Newport, Kentucky Turnhall, consisting of the Cincinnati, Cleveland and Dayton, Ohio Turner Societies and the Newport and Covington, Kentucky Turner Societies. The previously formed Columbus Turners had disbanded due to severe nativism, but it regrouped three years later with help from Gustav Tafel. Newport Turner Mitchfelder served as first president of the district, and Friedrich Bertsch served as its first secretary.[115]

By the time of the Turnerbund Convention in Washington, D.C, in 1865, Hamilton, Piqua and Ripley, Ohio Turners; Louisville, Kentucky Turners; and Terre Haute, Indiana Turners had joined the Cincinnati District. This Cincinnati District gained and lost a variety of member societies in southern Ohio over its many years.[116]

Ripley, Ohio, had a Turnverein from at least 1861 to 1865 that was briefly a part of the Cincinnati District. Ripley was an Ohio River town known to be a hotbed of Underground Railroad activity with residents like Reverend John Rankin. Miamisburg and Piqua, Ohio—south and north of Dayton, Ohio—had Turnvereine at this time that were associated with the Cincinnati District, as did Portsmouth and Portland, Ohio. The Chillicothe "Socialist" Turnverein had been founded on December 15, 1852, by L. Schneider and ten young men after Schneider visited a Turner district meeting in Cincinnati, Ohio. However, they never joined the Cincinnati District or the National Turnerbund.[117]

By the time of the National Convention in Louisville, Kentucky, in May 1872, an Ohio Valley District had been formed that included Dayton and Columbus, Ohio; Louisville, Kentucky; and Lafayette and Indianapolis, Indiana. The Cincinnati District included Covington, Cincinnati, Newport and the newly formed Cumminsville Turners, who sent their president, Carl Haebe, as their delegate to the conference.[118]

The following were other German-populated cities in Ohio that had Turnvereine that joined the Cincinnati District: Sandusky, Ohio, founded in September 1882 by President August Fettel (1884–95); Springfield, Ohio (1885–94); Lima, Ohio (1888); Hamilton, Ohio (1853–66, and 1890–96); Ohio Voerwarts (1889–92); Belmont, Ohio (1889–93); Newark, Ohio (1889–95); Tiffin, Ohio (1889–95); Dayton Voerwarts (1884–91);

Germania Turners in Findley, Ohio (1893–95); and Concordia Turners in Fostoria, Ohio (1894).[119]

On August 8, 1916, a curious new but short-term addition to the Ohio District Turners was the Deutsche Ungarische Turngemeinde of Cincinnati (or the German-Hungarian Turner Association), which was led by instructor John Pisch.[120] This organization reflected the new pre–World War I influx of mostly Catholic Donauschwab immigrants who would eventually form the Cincinnati Donauschwaben Society.

The district became headquartered in the specific Turner Society at which its president was a member. The districts hosted *tagsatzung*, or conventions, where they set the focus of the organization for the year. In the 1890s, the Ohio District was headquartered in the West End. It then shifted to Dayton from 1900 to 1905, North Cincinnati Turners in the 1910s, Newport from 1925 to 1927 and finally Covington in the 1930s. Today the local district is headquartered in Indianapolis, Indiana, and the American Turners are headquartered in Louisville, Kentucky.

The executives of the Ohio Turner District in 1899–1900. *From left to right*: Albert Remde, Cultural Education Committee; Fredrich Bertsch, corresponding secretary; Carl Ziegler, Physical Education Committee; G.F. Schweitzer, protocol secretary; William Riedlin, treasurer; Ekhardt Keller, Education Committee; Robert C. Georgi, president; Gustav Eckstein, Physical Education Committee; Fritz Wiessler, vice-president; and Nicholaus Seuss, district physical director. *Courtesy of Linda Houston, Covington Turners.*

After the Civil War, German Turner life in Cincinnati resumed. Lively events, debates and entertainments were hosted at the Turnhall. Cincinnati Turners participated in the German beer hall culture downtown and in the hill suburbs. Wielerts Saloon was owned by Cincinnati Turner Louis Wielert, the fitness instructor for several years before the Civil War. It became a place of politics, entertainment and musical concerts. Wielerts was located on the Walnut Street side of the Cincinnati Turnhall, and Cincinnati politicos like Boss George Cox, a North Turner, had regular tables here to have "runners" bring back news from political discussions happening at the Turnhall.

Atlantic Gardens, a popular bar, music and billiards hall at 245 Vine Street, was run by Cincinnati Turner John Lederer. It had concerts every night and matinees on Sundays. In 1904, John had the world's first electric organ built in Freiburg, Germany, specifically for Atlantic Gardens. Federer also took over another beer hall, Pacific Gardens.[121] The Belleview House, the Lookout House and the Price Hill House were also favorite Turner hangouts.

The organization that became the American Federation of Labor was organized at the Pittsburgh, Pennsylvania Turnhall on November 15–18, 1881. At the height of the labor movement in 1886, Cincinnati Germans and Turners had heard anarchist Albert E. Parsons speak at the Belleview House in Clifton before the Haymarket Riots in Chicago, Illinois, that year. Many cities across America staged protest parades after the Haymarket Riots. However, Cincinnati Central Turners and West End Turners pulled out at the last minute of the May Day Parade in Cincinnati on Sunday, May 2, 1886, the day after the eight-hour workday was supposed to be enacted for all U.S. businesses. Although Cincinnati Turners were members of the trade unions and supported improving conditions, hours and wages, they did not want to be connected to the Haymarket Riot anarchists.[122]

Politicians knew the importance of the German vote in Ohio, particularly in Columbus and Cincinnati. As a result, politicians became connected to the Turners. The Cincinnati Turners used their social connections to lobby for physical education in the public school system and to help elect progressive candidates. In June 1876, three hundred delegates from nearly every state in the country representing the German Republicans held a convention in the Cincinnati Turnhall to discuss reform candidates like those who had recently overthrown the Tammany Hall agents of corruption in New York City.[123]

A few successful presidential candidates wrote to American Turnvater Friedrich Hecker in Illinois to ask how to win the German vote—Abraham Lincoln in 1854 and Rutherford B. Hayes in 1876, asking him as a speaker

This is an advertisement for a Turner masked ball, a yearly event to celebrate Fasching, a German holiday similar to Mardi Gras. Elaborate costumes were worn, like that of General Bismarck, George and Martha Washington, "Onkel Sam" and Mataafa, a Samoan king.

with Ohio Germans.[124] Lincoln even owned a German-language newspaper in Ohio.

In the 1880s and 1890s, the Turnhall was host to political and nonpolitical conventions in the city. Turners promoted the secret ballot, the referendum, the direct election of U.S. senators by the people and proportional representation. They also supported women's suffrage and vigorously fought against prohibition.

President William Howard Taft recognized the importance of the German vote and became a member of the Central Turners before becoming president. Even though he had a wealthy Anglican ancestry, Taft's mother hired a German nanny to expose her children to German culture and the language of politics in Cincinnati. The Tafts' Unitarian background was very similar to the open-mindedness preached at Turnhalls. Taft's wife, Nellie Herron Taft, breaking Anglo-American society rules, loved to go to the German saloons to drink German lager and play cards.

This 1909 *Los Angeles Times* cartoon lampoons the portly President Taft exercising in his Turner uniform in the Cincinnati Turnhall.

Baseball has long been part of the Cincinnati Turner DNA. August "Gary" Hermann (1859–1931) was a formidable Central Turner because of his connection to national sports, including baseball, as well as local Cincinnati politics. Throughout his life, he practiced the "three Bs": bossism, baseball and bowling. Born in Germany, he made his start in Cincinnati as a typesetter for a local printer. The shop printed the official newspaper of the Hamilton County Courts, *The Law Bulletin*, and Hermann soon became involved in Cincinnati's political machine, rising in the ranks of the Ohio

Republican Party and even becoming one of political boss George B. Cox's most important men. Hermann became known for his flamboyant checkered clothes and for traveling with large entourages of people. He was the self-proclaimed sausage-eating champion of the world.[125]

In 1902, after Cox and the North Turner Fleischmann family purchased the Cincinnati Reds baseball club, they made Hermann club president. Hermann managed the club's concessions, which included Coca-Cola Company, Fleischmann Company, Jung Brewing Company and Philip Morris products. Over the next two decades, Hermann was arguably the most powerful man in American sports. He chaired Organized Baseball's National Commission, negotiated the beginning of the modern World Series, experimented with nighttime baseball and was a national leader in the American Bowling Congress. Hermann was on the Cincinnati Board of Education and on the city's board of administration and was chairman of Cincinnati's Water Works Commission, managing the construction of the waterworks known at its completion as the best in the nation.[126]

The Cincinnati Turners started their own banks to help one another out in business and homeownership. Many banks run by Anglo-Americans discriminated against new German immigrants, and it became hard for them to get home or even business loans. In order to support their own, the Cincinnati German community formed Bauvereine (Building and Loan Societies). These were German-owned private banks where members would buy shares into the society and borrow against their shares.

This photo is of Cincinnati Central Turner August Gary Hermann, president of the Cincinnati Reds, founder of the World Series and chairman of the 1909 Cincinnati National Turnfest.

In the 1880s, the Cincinnati Turners formed Turner Bauverein No. 3 to help their downtown members become homeowners. Turner Julius Engelke was president, Wilhelm Authenreith was treasurer and Max Burgheim was secretary. Several Turner-run building and loan companies existed in Cumminsville from 1871 into the 1900s, including the Workingmen German's Building and Savings Company, incorporated on May 26, 1882, and

This is the 1912–1916 Central Turners softball team champs. Top row, second from left, is Bill Liebling, the longest-standing member of the Central Turners.

This is the 1953 baseball team of the Cincinnati Central Turners. *Courtesy of Cincinnati Central Turners.*

the Twenty-fifth Ward German Building and Savings Company, incorporated on April 1, 1880. The West End Turner Building Company was incorporated on July 25, 1883, to help West End Turners. The idea caught on to non-German groups, and by the turn of the twentieth century, there were 374 building and loan companies in Cincinnati.[127]

Julius Engelke was born in 1839 in Hartzberg, Prussia, to wealthy Protestant parents. He came to America in 1854 and started his own saddler business. He was a Cincinnati Turner for more than twenty-five years, during which time he served several terms as president, spent eight years on the city council and was a member of Fire Company No. 2 on George Street.[128]

Max Burgheim (1844–1918) was a Central Turner and author of six books on Cincinnati German history. His best-known work, *Cincinnati in Wort und Bild* (*Cincinnati in Word and Picture*), published in 1888, was an encyclopedic work on Cincinnati German institutions and biographies of leading German citizens, many of whom were Cincinnati Turners.[129]

Henry Stueve (1835–1894), a West End Turner, was active in Cincinnati politics in 1877 and 1878, becoming the state senator from Hamilton County in 1888. He was president of Sonne Bauverein No. 1 and Grand Central Bauvereine No. 1 and 2 and was the first vice-president of the Ohio State Association of Bauvereine.[130]

Central Turner Benjamin Weik was the founder of the Eleventh Ward Bauverein, and Central Turner Charles Kuhl was president of the Harugari Bauverein, one of the oldest in Cincinnati. Leopold Kleybolte (1841–1928), North Turner, was president of the Western German Bank in 1900, and Covington Turner William Riedlin Jr. was vice-president of the Kentucky branch of that bank in 1908.

Cincinnati had several Turner mayors during the Progressive Era. Central and North Turner Gustav Tafel became Democratic mayor from 1897 to 1900. North and Covington Turner John Galvin (1862–1922) became mayor in 1909 upon the death of then mayor Leopold Markbreit, and then again from 1918 to 1921, during which time he helped to secure the presidential nomination of Warren G. Harding in 1920. North Turner Julius Fleischmann became Republican mayor from 1900 to 1905.

Cincinnati Central Turner physical instructor Carl Kroh started the annual Turner Exhibition at Music Hall in 1880, which lasted more than fifty-five years. This institution was taken over by successors Gustav Eckstein and later William P. Beyer. Each exhibition included performances of international dances by the children and complex gymnastic demonstrations by the older actives. During the war years, exhibitions became grand patriotic displays.

A female Turner group whose members were part of the yearly exhibition at Music Hall in the 1920s, when Dr. Gustav Eckstein was the instructor. *Courtesy of Cincinnati German Heritage Museum.*

In 1914, Turnhall manager Adolph Broetzler (1868–1936) billed the Turnhall as "the largest halls for balls, entertainments, weddings, parties, mass meetings, and conventions." A total of forty-five German societies held regular meetings at this hall. The job of Turnhall manager was very important to the organization—hall rental income was one of its largest sources of revenue.

The Cincinnati Central, Covington and North Cincinnati Turners participated in gymnastics exhibitions at the 1928 Pure Food and Health Show at the Cincinnati Zoo from August 26 to September 9. Twenty-four active Central Turners in gold lamé lederhosen costumes performed on August 31 to roaring applause. This show was sponsored by the Cincinnati Retail Grocers Association and was filled with entertainment galore, including musical performances and vaudeville acts. This exhibition was the first time that many Cincinnatians had ever witnessed Turner gymnastics.[131]

Also in 1928, the Ohio District Turners produced from their Forty-seventh District Convention a "how-to" handbook for organizing, running and managing a Turner organization. Presidents and physical instructors of the Cincinnati, Dayton, Newport and Covington Turners contributed articles on all aspects of the Turner organization. William Streit, president of the Ohio District, said about the handbook, "This is Ohio's contribution to the modern Turner thought and we offer this symposium as a challenge to other Districts to likewise contribute in fair measure to the advancement and understanding of our Turner activities."[132]

Cincinnati Turner Bears

The Cincinnati Turner organization grew with a man as he aged. It started with Zoeglingsverein (a young children's class), and then came the knabenklasse (boys's class), out of which young men grew into active Turners. As a man aged, he became a member of the Baeren-Reige (Bear Regiment), sometimes called the Business Men's class. Bears were older Turners, usually above the age of thirty-five. The term originated because older Turner men looked like bears and had more barrel-shaped bodies as compared to the thin gymnasts of the active class. The organization was originally developed to provide a venue for older Turners to continue their athletic endeavors

The bear class of the Cincinnati Central Turners in 1948. *Courtesy of Cincinnati Central Turners.*

after they reached an age where they could no longer compete as actives in their society.

The Turner bears held their own meetings, called *Commerz*, and usually had a hangout in their respective Turnhall that they called the Bear Den. They elected their own executive bears and even competed in Turnfests and local exhibitions (Volksfests). There was an element of Mark Twain humor in all communication about the local bears. Officers were *oberbear* (chief bear or president), *unterbear* (vice-president), *kratzbear* (literally scratchbear or secretary), *tanzenbear* (literally dancing bear or Turner instructor), *financebear* and *treasurybear*.

The bears became an important part of support for the Turner classes. The Ohio District bears for many years held New Year's receptions, exercises and parties at the Covington Turnhall. Turner William Riedlin presided over these events and christened all new bears into the group with his original Baden cowbell. North Turner Morris Mohr even hosted a super bear class for early risers or third-shift workers, held from 1:00 a.m. to 2:00 a.m. every morning at the Corryville Turnhall.[133]

FEMALE TURNERS AND LADIES' AUXILIARIES

Nearly every Turner Society in America formed Damenvereine or Schwestervereine—Women's Auxiliaries or Sister Associations. These auxiliaries were a great benefit to fundraising and event planning for the organizations. Married women had their own gym classes, as did single women and young girls. The Women's Auxiliary of the Cincinnati Central Turners was founded on November 11, 1887, after the earlier auxiliary from 1850 had become inactive. The Cumminsville Turners founded their Damenverein in 1884 and the North Turners in 1886. Covington Turners had formed theirs in 1856 and again in 1899 after years of inactivity. Unfortunately, there are no specific references to a West End or Norwood Turner Ladies' Auxiliary, but they certainly both had one to support their respective organizations.

The Newport Turners had a Damenverein in 1856 that aided during the *Pfingsmontag* Riot in Covington and helped the Central Turner Damenverein during the Civil War making bandages, knitting socks and providing many other comforts for the men on the front. They jointly prepared and served the "welcome home" banquet at the Central Turnhall after the Turner soldiers returned. After years of inactivity, a new Women's Auxiliary was founded in 1912.

The Dayton, Ohio Turners formed a Women's Auxiliary in 1913 that became the last remnant of the Dayton Turners. When their Turner husbands passed away, they stuck together as a card group and oversaw the merging with the Dayton Liederkranz in 1952.

The American Turnerbund formed a National Women's Auxiliary in 1919 at the Twenty-seventh National Turner Convention in Louisville, Kentucky. Its primary fundraising activities went toward supporting the Turner Normal College and the National Turner Camp Brosius, as well as supporting active Turners who found themselves unable to pay their yearly dues. The Greater Cincinnati Turner Women's Auxiliary played a very active role throughout the life of the national organization. Elizabeth Bachmann of the Newport Turners was second vice-president in 1921, Mrs. Printz of Cincinnati was first vice-president in 1929 and Louella Roth of Covington Turners was treasurer in 1948. Laura Olt, wife of Dayton, Ohio Turner president Fred Olt, was very active in the organization, serving as treasurer in 1929 and president in 1937.

Like the bears, the Women's Auxiliaries also employed an element of Mark Twain humor in their social events. When the Covington Women's Auxiliary celebrated its fifty-fifth anniversary in 1954, the ladies from Dayton and Cincinnati came by bus to the Covington Turnhall to help celebrate. "We will never forget Dayton unloading from the bus. Hats of all descriptions, shapes and sizes were about all you could see. For example—a hat trimmed with pretzels, one brimmed with an arrangement of hen eggs."[134]

Although the majority of Cincinnati Turner instructors for female Turners were men, the women's auxiliaries offered sewing, needlepoint and other home management classes to help young girls prepare to manage a German household. In addition, the women's auxiliaries taught the Turner philosophy of keeping a sound mind in a sound body, fighting a then prevailing American Protestant mindset that female exercise was immoral. Turner men were supportive of the women in their life, inviting them to attend the debates and celebratory events and supporting the women's suffrage movement. Many Cincinnati Turner daughters were educated at the Turner Normal College and encouraged to start independent careers as physical education instructors and public school teachers before marrying.

To celebrate the one-hundred-year anniversary of Jahn's founding of the first turnplatz near Berlin, Germany, the Cincinnati and Covington Turners dedicated a monument to him in Clifton's Imwood Park on October 22, 1911, carved by sculptor Leopold Fettweis Jr. Imwood Park had been the site of many Turner picnics and events, like the 1873 national Turnfest.

This 1911 photo shows the Cincinnati Central Turners at the dedication of the Jahn Memorial at Imwood Park in Corryville. *Courtesy of Cincinnati Central Turners.*

Standing ten feet high, seven feet wide and three feet thick and weighing thirty thousand pounds, the monument (made out of New Westerly granite) is ornamented with a storm-beaten German oak and an Italian marble bust of Turnvater Jahn. Each year in May, the Turners and United Singers of Cincinnati paid homage with ceremonies at the monument, until the rise of anti-German sentiment during World War I. Then trees and shrubbery were planted around the monument to obscure it from view. Central Turner instructor Carl Ziegler, in preparation for the seventy-fifth anniversary of Jahn's death in 1927, had the trees removed to bring the monument back into full view.[135]

The Turners made it through the rebirth of anti-German sentiment of World War I, but the Great Depression period between 1929 and 1944 was really the end to many Turner Societies across the nation as funds became scarce to support and maintain them. It was during this period that American Turners lost more than one-third of their membership and societies. Locally, only Central Turners, Covington Turners and Dayton Turners made it through this period. West Turners, North Turners and Norwood Turners were all victims of the depression and prohibition.

By 1933, the rise of the Nazi regime in Germany had added another challenge for the Cincinnati and National Turner organizations. At the 1933

National Convention in Elkhart Lake, Wisconsin, the delegates adopted a resolution of opposition to the Nazi regime and its suppression of free press, freedom of conscience and the right of assembly. The Nazi government had confiscated property, dissolved the organization and imprisoned leaders of the Arbeiter Turnerbund of Germany. The last Turnfest before World War II was held in 1928 in Cologne, as Hitler banned Turnfests. The convention delegates also stated in the resolution that they were "very sorry that the German Turnerschaft found it necessary to submit to the tyrannical edicts of the German regime," distancing themselves from Nazi-occupied Germany. William Beyer, physical instructor of Cincinnati Central Turners; Alban Wolff, president of Covington Turners; George Roth, physical instructor of Covington Turners; and Fred Olt, president of the Dayton Turners, were present at the convention to ratify this resolution.[136]

In 1938, the Turners prepared for another wave of anti-German hysteria. The American Turnerbund changed its name to the American Turners. In the 1940s, the Central Turners hosted American Legion Post No. 636 at the Turnhall downtown to proclaim their patriotism and avoid suspicion. Cincinnati Turners once again did themselves proud, with large representation of the best physically trained men for enlisting in the service. World War II statistics showed that 93.2 percent of the American Turners examined for services were found to be physically fit versus the general average of 66.8 percent.

This is the 100th anniversary commemorative Turner stamp, issued in Cincinnati, Ohio, on November 21, 1948. *Courtesy of Cincinnati Central Turners.*

To commemorate the 100th anniversary of the founding of the Turners in America, a U.S. postal stamp was designed by Alvin R. Meissner, chief designer of the U.S. Bureau of Engraving. Meissner was an honorary fifty-year member of the Detroit Turners. The stamp features the Roman discus thrower, the American Turner emblem, embellished by a laurel wreath symbolizing honor. A run of 60 million of these stamps was issued, and they were placed on sale on the founding date

This 1950s photo shows a Turner gymnastics group practicing at the Walnut Street Central Turnhall. *Left to right*: Janet Boland, John Mohr, Betty Memmel, Harry Roberts and Irene Schoeiber. *Courtesy of Indiana University–Purdue University Indianapolis (IUPUI).*

of November 21, 1948, in Cincinnati, Ohio, the birthplace of the Turner movement. At the occasion of the first sale was Anton J. Stoss, president of Cincinnati Turners; Carl Wiedemann, national Turner president; and Robert Fellers, U.S. Post Office superintendent of stamps.[137]

By the 1950s, the Central Turnhall, nearing one hundred years old, was deteriorating and becoming expensive to keep up. Alterations had been made in 1890, adding a new and larger gym, dressing and bathing facilities and a large hall over the gym. In 1923, after buying up an old ground lease that was expiring, ten bowling alleys on the third floor were added, along with a post office on the first floor. A 1927 façade restoration program designed to boost tenant rentals failed because of the depression. The Turners even bought land on Vine and Shields Streets to build a new Turnhall, but that plan failed due to the hall's proximity to the North Turnhall in Corryville, and the property was sold. A fire in January 1948 destroyed the bowling alleys and other parts of the Turnhall. The restoration without the bowling alleys seriously strained the organization. The German clubs that had provided sources of rental income for the hall had moved to the suburbs. The Central Turners even rented the gym to diving teams in the late 1950s to practice on trampolines during the winter.

This 1940s photo shows a male and two female Turners exhibiting a parallel bar formation in the Walnut Street Central Turnhall. *Courtesy of Cincinnati Central Turners.*

Above: This 1920s photo shows a Turner outing with retired instructor Gustav Eckstein in center, seated, and then current instructor William P. Beyer seated on the ground. *Courtesy of Cincinnati German Heritage Museum.*

Below: The Cincinnati Turner basketball team, who were Cincinnati champions from 1904 to 1905. *Courtesy of Cincinnati Central Turners.*

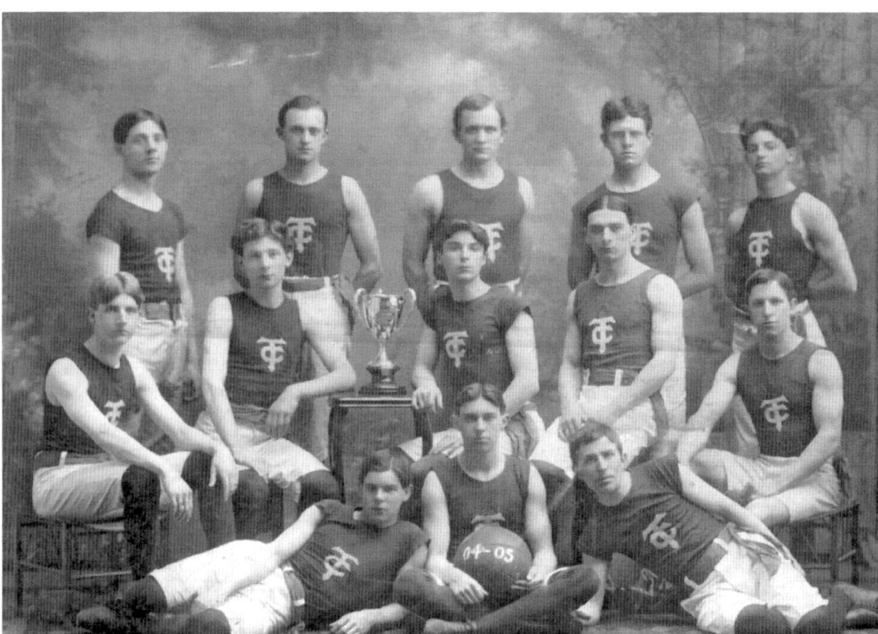

Above: This 1950s photo shows a Central Turner group practicing for an exhibition. *Left to right*: George Mueller, William Kamleiter Sr., Elsie Durand, William Liebing, Al Bashang, Rosella Wendt, Frieda Hug and Edna Eisermann. *Courtesy of Indiana University–Purdue University Indianapolis (IUPUI).*

Below: The Cincinnati Central Turners volleyball champions of 1926. *From left to right*: William Kammleiter, William Oberman, George Goldfus, William Beyer (instructor), William Liebling, Andrew Hug and Leo Langen. *Courtesy of Cincinnati German Heritage Museum.*

In 1959, the Cincinnati Central Turners bought land in Springfield Township on Pinney Lane and moved the organization to the farthest suburb outside the limits of Cincinnati. The old Turnhall downtown was razed in 1972, leaving an open lot. The Pinney Lane building was small, so a new building was built. It does not have a gymnasium, but it serves as a hall for meetings, dances and special events.

The benefit of the Pinney Lane property was its amount of open land. It housed a fishing lake and enough land to build baseball diamonds. A Fourth of July drag softball game called the "Skirt Game" was a popular event for many years in the 1990s. A Turner Casting Club was formed, and it also became a popular sport among members.

In 1959, activities included Saturday night bingo socials, anniversary dinners and dances, New Year's Eve celebrations, season closing socials and four men's teams in the Detroit National Bowling Tournament. There was also a youth baseball team in the local Babe Ruth League.

Since 1963, the American Turners have had a Turner National Golf Tournament, of which Cincinnati Central Turners have been active participants. In 2008, Art Flowers of Central Turners was presented the Red

The current Cincinnati Central Turnhall at Pinney Lane in Springfield Township.

Top Davis Award at this tournament. It was named in memory of Wayne "Red Top" Davis of the Fort Wayne Turners and was established to honor members who best represent a sound mind in a sound body and a sense of fair play and fun. Art has attended the golf tournament for thirty-six years.

William Liebling (1888–1988), a Cincinnati Central Turner for eighty-one years, holds the record for the oldest participating Cincinnati Turner member. A jeweler and diamond broker in downtown, Liebling was an active Turner, participating in many exhibitions at Music Hall and in several national Turnfests. He played semiprofessional baseball in Florida and never married. He left a generous endowment to the Cincinnati Central Turners.[138]

The Cincinnati Central Turners today are led by President Marlene Lintz and strive to promote the Turner ideals to the next generation of American youth.

The Cumminsville Turnverein

Tolerance against all fanaticism.
—Turner constitution

The Cumminsville Turners were the first suburban Cincinnati Turner group founded from the Central Turners. Under the influence of Wilhelm Sanders, they banded together on August 6, 1870, and stayed together for nearly twenty-five years.[139] Even though they were the first offshoot Cincinnati Turner organization and one of the most prominent for many years, they have been all but forgotten to history. Several of the early founders and organization's presidents were Cincinnati Turners, and many were Civil War veterans. One of the first founders, Joe Eiselein, was the son of one of the original founders of the Cincinnati Turnverein in 1848. Another founder and first president was Wilhelm Sanders, a veteran of the Ninth Ohio Regiment during the war. Carl Haebe, a president, was also a veteran of the Ninth Ohio and a Cincinnati Turner. Louis Heuser, who served as first lieutenant of Company A of the Ninth Ohio, transferred from the Cincinnati Turners to Cumminsville in 1876. Fred Dorman (1820–1880) was a Cincinnati Turner before moving to Cumminsville in 1866 to open his tavern, the Dorman House.

The group spanned the gamut of German socioeconomic standing. Members were brewers, carpenters, railway workers, tailors, shop owners, frame makers, doctors, pharmacists and hotel and saloon proprietors. They represented nearly all the kingdoms of what we now know as the united

The Cumminsville Turnverein in front of their hall on Hoffner Street, with their ribbons from the 1889 Bundesturnfest in Cincinnati. Representing many extended family groups, the majority were members of the Apple Street German Evangelical Church.

country of Germany. Even though the customs from these regions were as varied as our own customs vary from state to state, what they shared was a somewhat common language that helped them to navigate this new land together. Many of the Cumminsville Turners were also Forty-eighters, although some did not share the extreme liberal mentality. Some were even second-generation German Americans. Like the other neighborhood Turner groups that would follow the forming of the Cumminsville Turners, they would have three things in common: connection to a neighborhood German Evangelical or Reformed Church (in this case the Apple Street German Evangelical Church); connection to a neighborhood brewery (in this case the John Caspar Bruckmann Brewery); and connection to a neighborhood park to celebrate organizational picnics and Turnfests (in this case Ludlow Grove, which was located conveniently out of Cincinnati city limits, exempt from its Sunday liquor laws).

The original founders of the Cumminsville Turners were as follows: Phillip Lorenz, a builder from Bavaria; John Caspar Bruckmann from Bavaria, owner of Bruckmann Brewery; August Ernst Gulow, tailor from Mecklenburg-Schwerin; Herman Krumpe, bridge builder from Prussia; Wilhelm Sanders (1854–1931), a carpenter from Bavaria; Ed Herberg, Cincinnati-born to Bavarian parents; Andreas Spaeth, student, with parents from Bavaria; Reuben Levy; Mattias Pfeffer; Caspar Tschus, a Civil War veteran; Christian Schamberger; Joe Eiselein, baker's apprentice; Franz Freitag, a laborer born to Bavarian parents; Adam Kraus, a student born to Baden parents; and Otto Woellert, a frame worker born in Cincinnati to parents from Mecklenburg-Schwerin.[140]

The majority of the members of the Cumminsville Turnverein were also members of the Apple Street German Evangelical Church, built in 1856. The Turnhall hosted choral concerts performed by the church choir and the Turner Society's Maennerchor, or Men's Chorus. Although early Cincinnati Turners were anti-congregational and anti-clerical, the German Evangelical Protestants formed a good compromise. Dedicated to religious liberty, evangelical Protestants stood for freedom of thought, open-mindedness and respect for those whose beliefs were different. Refusing to join a larger synod, the German American Evangelical Protestant Church had three common ideals: they believed in freedom of thought, conscience and interpretation in points of doctrinal difference; they believed in the autonomy of each congregation—memories of their lives in Europe, where churches were often controlled by the state, inspired this ideal; and finally, they believed in the authority of the laity over the pastor, where congregations, not the pastor, made the decisions. Each congregation had to solve its own problems. This made for a liberal-minded community that espoused the Turner principles of "sound mind in a sound body."

Cumminsville was Cincinnati's first commuter suburb. With its passenger depot for the Cincinnati, Hamilton and Dayton Railroad, Cumminsville's residents could commute to good and stable factory jobs in the city but also enjoy the cleaner air and less cramped conditions of the country. There are numerous references that Cumminsvillians felt that the Cincinnati streetcars weren't properly equipped for the service to their neighborhood and that they were charged expensive fares.

The Cumminsville Turners met first at Streng's Hall and then rented a dry goods store at no. 293 in C.C. Williams Subdivision on the street north next to Dirr Street, now in the path of the Interstate 74 interchange at Colerain Avenue. They finally built a large Turnhall on Hoffner Street, designed by Mr. Boetter, that was finished in early November 1872 after only four months of construction.[141] This Turnhall was large enough to house during the 1889 Turnfest delegates from Newport, Covington and West, North and Central Cincinnati Turners, as well as Sandusky, Dayton, Lima and Columbus, Ohio Turners, for a district meeting and celebration.

J.W. Streng, who lent his hall to the Turners while they were building their own hall, was a butcher from Bavaria. Born there in 1821, he arrived in Cincinnati in July 1849, moving to Cumminsville in 1853. In addition to his butchery, he operated Streng's Hall, a boardinghouse, with his German immigrant wife, Barbara Gensendoefer, and their four children. One of his sons, Andrew, a Turner, was a jeweler on Colerain Avenue.

The presidents of the Cumminsville Turnverein were Wilhelm Sanders (1870–72), Conrad Soellheim (1872), Carl Haebbe (1879–84), Leopold Dressel (1885–87) and August Ernst Gulow (1873–78; 1889–94).[142]

One of the first presidents of the Cumminsville Turnverein was Dr. Conrad Soellheim. Born in Bavaria in 1836, his father was a prominent physician. Receiving a high school education, he came to America in 1853, practicing medicine in Dubois County, Indiana, for five years. He came to Cincinnati in 1858 and later, in 1861, graduated from the Cincinnati College of Medicine and Surgery, where he became demonstrator of anatomy. At the breakout of the Civil War, Dr. Soellheim enlisted in the Ninth Ohio Infantry as an assistant surgeon for about eighteen months. During the war, he was a brigade surgeon and also surgeon in charge of the Union field hospital at Chattanooga, Tennessee, managing six physicians and fifteen orderlies. Soellheim recorded the peril of this wartime field triage medicine in his diary in Chattanooga:

> *All day countless ambulances arrived loaded with wounded. The scene was indescribable. We could not start amputating until the morning of the 20th after which we had done what critical to minimal care for the many injured. But by 9:30…fresh fighting raged near us. We were soon under artillery bombardment. Then an order came from the chief physician. I was to take all the severely wounded with me in ambulances to Rossville, about 10 miles off. The rest of the wounded, those not badly hurt, were to walk there. Too late! The battle already threatened the hospital. Refugees, the wounded and the dying crowded around us, enemy infantry stormed at us…Ghastly chaos! Then came the new wounded. In rebel hands, very many of our officers and men, lacking care and proper treatment had died of wounds. With us too, far more of the injured perished than should have perished for lack of nourishing food and much else.*[143]

Soellheim settled in Cumminsville on Cherry Street, practicing medicine and being very active in the Cumminsville Turnverein. He lectured throughout the community and at Freethinker gatherings. In April 1879, the *Northside Transcript* reported that "Dr. Soelheim will give a very interesting lecture on geology next Tuesday at Odd Fellows Hall [on Hamilton Avenue], to which the public is invited." His second wife, Minnie, referred to in Cumminsville as "Madam Soellheim," was the local diva voce, singing the part of Frau von Langsalm in the Cumminsville Turner Maennerchor's five-act production of *Der Wirrwarr!*, by August von Kotzebue, at Streng's Hall.[144]

Soellheim was one of the few members of the Cumminsville Turners who had very liberal-minded Forty-eighter views. He was associated with the Freethinkers and was even referred to by the *Northside Transcript* as an "infidel"—a term associated with the Freethinkers—when an article about his divorce from his third wife was printed. The majority of the Cumminsville Turners were not as liberally minded as Soellheim, and that is perhaps why he only lasted one year as the organization's president. Soellheim would relocate to South Perry, Ohio, to continue practicing medicine.

Karl Haebe became a Cumminsville Turner in 1877 and was president from 1879 to 1884. He had joined the Newport Turners in 1855 and volunteered with the Ninth Ohio Regiment, Company A, before moving to Cumminsville.[145] Karl co-owned a cornice works business at 4032 Hamilton Avenue with Fredrick Blickle from 1869 to 1890; Karl's son, Louis, also a Cumminsville Turner, was employed there.[146] Karl was remembered by his Civil War comrades in their history: "Who does not remember yet the pleasant times in the gunboat, a tent covered with tin, led in song by Ernst Koegel, Charles Klintworth, and Karl Haebe. Full voiced, jolly comrades, they provided choral leadership but only after always providing good libations."[147]

President Leopold Dressel (1857–1929) emigrated from Coburg, Germany, and was a pharmacist. After his term as president with Cumminsville Turners ended in late 1887, he moved with his wife, Marie, and daughters, Linda, Ella and Helen, to Norwood to construct its first drugstore at 4336 Montgomery Road, opposite the Norwood Public Library.

The longest-standing president of the Cumminsville Turnverein was August Ernst Gulow (1837–1901), an immigrant from Penzlin, Duchy of Mecklenburg-Schwerin. He was a merchant tailor on Hamilton Avenue, president of the Workingmen's Building and Loan and a Cincinnati councilman. His brother, Wilhelm C. Gulow (1833–1913), with whom he immigrated in 1857, was a member of the West End Turners. Gulow Street, a one-block street west of Hamilton Avenue in Northside, remains as a tribute to this Cumminsville Turner president.

"Professor" August Robert Gulow (1860–1947), son of August E. Gulow and a Cumminsville Turner, was the physical instructor of the Cincinnati Police Department and superintendent of its gymnasium from

June 6, 1894, into the early 1900s. He was also physical instructor for the Cumminsville Turners from 1892 to 1894, and his position was filled in 1894 by Erich Bergmann, who lived at 1640 Hoffner near the Turnhall. Gulow won a number of medals in Turner athletic contests and was an expert wrestler, sparrer and fencer. Gulow was popular in the police force for his boxing and self-defense lessons and was known as a "great reader and an intelligent man."[148]

Erich Bergmann was the last physical instructor of the Cumminsville Turners, from 1894 to 1896. His father, Gustav Bergmann, a veteran of the Ninth Ohio, Company A, was a teacher in the public schools of Cincinnati and had joined the Dayton, Ohio Turners in 1856 after emigrating to America in 1855.[149] By 1907, Erich was teacher of the Sixteenth District and Intermediate Cincinnati Public Schools and in 1903 was the secretary for the Ohio Turner District and a member of the North Cincinnati Turners.

August Robert Gulow, Cumminsville Turner instructor from 1892 to 1894 and Cincinnati police physical instructor from 1894 to 1900. A street sign in Northside honors him and his father, August Ernst Gulow, president of the Cumminsville Turners.

A Women's Auxiliary was founded in 1884, and the members made the flag that flew over the Turnhall. Many German seamstresses who were wives, daughters and nieces of the Cumminsville Turners could have made the flag. Cumminsville was known for having a large number of merchant tailors, dressmakers and milliners and was Cincinnati's fashion mecca from the 1880s until after the turn of the twentieth century.[150]

The Cumminsville Turnhall hosted meetings of other clubs associated with the Turners, like the Cumminsville Raucher

Casino, Cumminsville Turner Maennerchor, Limburger Cheese Group, Grant Club and the Northside Fishing Club. The Cumminsville Raucher Casino (or Smoking Casino) was an interesting club. Many Cincinnati German neighborhoods had their own Raucher Casinos. Men met to smoke their long German pipes and play cards. The "casino" designation didn't necessarily mean that there was betting for money, and in most cases, if there was betting, proceeds would go to some benevolent organization like an orphanage or widows' home. An outdoor beer garden, for which they raised $2,000 over two years, was added to the Turnhall in 1889, had a privacy fence, tables and chairs and was rentable for parties.[151]

Before their Hoffner Street hall was completed in November 1872, the Cumminsville Turners hosted the Grant Club, for those backing the election of Ulysses S. Grant, at Streng's Hall. The opposing club, the Greely Club, was run by a German non-Turner, Julius Markgraf, whose father ran the Markgraf Saloon at 4032 Hamilton Avenue, next to Turner Theodore Woellert's frame shop and family home. Clearly the majority of the German vote was in favor of Grant.

One of the first events the Cumminsville Turners hosted at their newly built Turnhall on Hoffner was a joint Christmas concert of the Cumminsville Turner Maennerchor and the Apple Street Evangelical Church Choir.[152] They also planned excursions by train to see German musical concerts and German theater in other cities.

The Cumminsville Turners celebrated their two-year anniversary on Saturday, August 2, 1872, at Ludlow Grove between St. Bernard and Bond Hill, arriving by canalboat on the Miami and Erie Canal, which went through Cumminsville, now the path of Interstate 75.[153] Until the mid-1930s, St. Bernard and Bond Hill was largely rural and was surrounded by orchards and dairy farms. The people of Cumminsville liked Ludlow Grove because it was out of police supervision of Cincinnati and thus outside of the "Sunday Blue Laws," designed to prevent Germans from their Sunday *gemütlichkeit*.

In 1884, Cumminsville hosted a *Stiftungsfest*, or local Turner event, at the Cumminsville Turnhall in 1884 that included Central Turners, West End Turners, North Turners and Lick Run Turners. Exhibiting their love of marching, the local Cincinnati Turners marched in three groups, all meeting at the Cumminsville Turnhall for the Turnfest. The Lick Run Turners marched three miles from their hall near Queen City Avenue to Cumminsville; the North Cincinnati Turners marched three miles direct from their hall on Vine Street to Cumminsville; and the Central Turners, joined by Newport and Covington Turners, marched a total of fifteen miles from Walnut Street to the West End Turnhall on Freeman Avenue and then, with the West End Turners, marched en masse to Cumminsville—a total of 150 marching Turners. What a spectacle that would have been, with each group's band and choirs singing—and, of course, drinking—along the way![154]

The Cumminsville Turnhall housed concerts by the Cumminsville Maennerchor, comedies, theater and benefit dances for associated organizations like the Streetcar Railway Employees Mutual Aid Society No. 2, and it even raised money for widows of members. Before social security, pensions and employee benefits, Turner Societies aided members by providing for these social loopholes not covered by the government. Also hosted were elaborate festivities like *Maskenball* (Masked Balls) to celebrate Fasching, the German version of Mardi Gras. Germans took these balls seriously, and elaborate paired costumes like George and Martha Washington and Night and Day were worn.

The 1883 Cumminsville Turner Family Christmas party was described in detail in the *Cincinnati Freie Presse*. The elegant club hall was decorated festively for the party with bunting, greens, emblems of the Turner Societies and the flags of the various states of Germany. A large Christmas tree was decorated and surrounded with many beautiful gifts—harmonicas, albums, picture books, game books, tricycles, children's games of all sorts and puppets and dolls. After several lively addresses, the dancing started, involving both the young and old, which lasted until "Aurora flew across the sky," announcing the dawn.[155]

The hall also housed lively political debates about local issues. In 1879, a lecture on the mass migration of African Americans to Kansas and the Colorado silver rush was hosted at the Turnhall.[156] In February 1880, it housed a rowdy meeting of the citizens of Cumminsville. City Solicitor Kumler, a former resident of Cumminsville, had put together a strong resolution demanding more water and less streetcar fare for the Twenty-fifth Ward of Cumminsville. This resolution stalled at city hall, angering Cumminsville citizens.[157]

At the various local, regional and national Turnfests hosted in Cincinnati, the Cumminsville Turners extended a brotherly hand of accommodation to out-of-town Turner Societies. The Cumminsville Turnhall became a dormitory for three hundred Turners for the 1889 Turnfest, and Cumminsville Turner George Elsasser housed two hundred in his own Dorman House.

When the Lick Run, West End and North Cincinnati Turner Societies were accepted into the Ohio District in 1884, Carl Haebe, Cumminsville

Turner president, addressed the meeting, calling them "der drei Liebling," or the three youngest kids.[158]

Like the Cincinnati Turner Societies, the Cumminsville Turners held strong ties to families and groups of chain immigrants from the same villages and regions. An example was a subgroup of families involved with the Cumminsville Turners: the "Penzlin Nine." These were nine families from the village of Penzlin in the Duchy of Mecklenburg-Schwerin who had immigrated to Cumminsville during the period of 1855–70. They consisted of the families of Theodore Woellert and Freda Burchard; Carl Dankert and Therese Burchard; Friedrich Sonnenburg and Bernhadina Burchard; Friedrich Dankert; August and Wilhelm Gulow; Johann Woeller (not Woellert); Carl and Theodore Hinborn; Heinrich Himburg; and August Graf.

Theodore Woellert was the first of the group to immigrate to Cincinnati, in 1855, moving to Cumminsville in 1859. Theodore's father, Johann Heinrich Woellert (1801–1859), and grandfather, Christian Friedrich Woellert (1770–1833), had been *jaegers*, or sharpshooters, who helped overthrow the Napoleonic forces occupying the Duchy of Mecklenburg-Schwerin.[159] Theodore immigrated to escape being one of these guards. He was a Forty-eighter of a different sort—a pacifist who immigrated to avoid serving for the monarchy. Given his family's military background with the Prussian army, Theodore Woellert and the other Penzlin Nine did not volunteer to fight in the Ninth Ohio Regiment in the Civil War. This was significant, given that four of the recruiting officers of the companies of the Ninth Ohio were from Mecklenburg-Schwerin: Ernst Rubenow, first lieutenant in Company D; Karl Joseph, captain of Company A; Louis Hauser, first lieutenant in Company A; and Wilhelm Heubing, first lieutenant of Company F. Karl Joseph had volunteered with the Schwerin Jaeger battalion in 1851, before immigrating, and was physical instructor in gymnastics, swordsmanship and swimming in the Mecklenburg cities of Schwerin and Rostock.[160]

For the Penzlin Nine group, practicality won out over principle. The men probably agreed with the reasons for entering into the Civil War but had come to America first and foremost to build a better life for their family. This meant that it was more important to manage their businesses and support their families rather than run off to the battlefield.

All of the Penzlin Nine were taught as young boys by one famous Forty-eighter, Eduard Rapp, the principal of the *Burgerschule* (Penzlin City School). Rapp immigrated in 1850 to Cleveland, Ohio, for asylum after contributing to the revolution of 1848 in Mecklenburg. When reporting

Rapp's immigration to America, the *Rostocker Abendblatt*, a newspaper in Mecklenburg, noted that "[t]he State of Ohio seems to be the promised land to many Mecklenburgers."[161]

Theodore Woellert Sr. established a career at the Catholic German-owned Nurre Picture Frame Company in downtown Cincinnati, where he worked his entire life. His two sons, Otto and Theodore Jr., both worked at Nurre for their entire lives and were founding active Turner members of the Cumminsville Turnverein, as well as members of the Apple Street German Evangelical Church. Theodore Woellert Sr. sponsored the immigration of Johann Woeller and the brothers Carl and Theodore Hinborn, who would also work at Nurre and also be involved in the Cumminsville Turners.[162] This was a very similar story for other groups of chain immigrants in Cincinnati. An early pioneer immigrated, became settled and then hosted other family members from the same village. The Turner Society was a way to preserve their culture and a great resource for connections to jobs and opportunities with other German members of the Turner organization who owned businesses.

The town of Penzlin had started its own Turner Society in 1864, called the Penzlin "Gut Heil" Turners, before the Woeller, Hinborn, Himburg and Graf families immigrated to Cumminsville in the 1870s, and may have been a motivating factor for the founding of the Cumminsville Turners in 1870. The Penzlin "Gut Heil" Turners celebrated a fiftieth anniversary in 1914 with a Turnfest for the surrounding villages' Turnvereine.[163] Penzlin is about 50 kilometers from Berlin, where Jahn is given the credit of founding the first Turner Society. Mecklenburg had numerous citizen militias and sharpshooters who helped to overthrow the Napoleonic forces. Additionally, the large capital city of Mecklenburg, Neubrandenburg, actually started a Turnverein in 1803 that predated Jahn's in Berlin by eight years. Two other large cities—Mecklenburg-Friedland (1812) and Neustrelitz (1816)—founded Turnvereine shortly after Jahn's in Berlin.[164] So the region from which the Penzlin Nine immigrated was a hotbed of Turner activity.

The Penzlin Nine also showed the family interconnectivity between Turner organizations. August E. Gulow's brother, Wilhelm, would settle in Cincinnati's West End and be a prominent member of the West End Turnverein. Otto Woellert's father-in-law, Friedrich Dhonau, a carriage maker in Cumminsville, was also a member of the Cumminsville Turners. Theodore Woellert Jr.'s wife, Carolina Henke, had family in other Cincinnati Turner Societies. Her Westphalian immigrant father, Johann Heinrich Henke, was a member of the North Cincinnati Turnverein and owned a boot and shoe shop near Washington Park in Over-the-Rhine. Carrie's uncle, Carl Spreen, a grocer, notary and realtor, was a member of the West End Turnverein.

John C. Bruckmann (1829–1887) was born in Berka, Thuringia, and was a founder of the Bruckmann Brewery in 1856 in Cumminsville. He served as city councilman in 1873 from Cumminsville, was a Turner and an Odd Fellow and was also president of the Workingman's Building and Loan Association in Cumminsville in the 1880s, an organization that helped many Cumminsville Turners and other Germans build their own houses, some of which are still standing.[165]

Many of the brewers at the Bruckmann Brewery were Cumminsville Turners. The brewing foreman, Heinrich Rennert, was a member of the Turnverein and the Cumminsville Raucher Casino, hosted at the Turnhall.[166] This tie to the neighborhood brewery made it convenient to serve Brucks beer at the Cumminsville Turner events.

Another leading member of the Cumminsville Turners who had great national influence on the American Turner movement was Oscar Sputh (1860–1932). Sputh was the Turner instructor for both the Cumminsville Turners and the Corryville Turners in 1889 and was on the judging committee of the July 27, 1890 Columbus Local Turnfest. He had immigrated to

Above, left: Cumminsville Turner Theodore E. Woellert Jr. proudly displays his 1889 Cincinnati Turnfest lapel pin in the lower-left panel of his lapel in this photo.

Above, right: This is a lithograph of John Caspar Bruckmann, founder of the Bruckmann Brewery in Cumminsville and one of the founding Cumminsville Turners.

Cincinnati from Saxony in 1878 with his brother, Christian Sputh (1850–1909), working as a brewer at Bruckmann Brewery in Cumminsville. Christian was a member of the Dayton, Ohio Turners from 1886 to 1908.[167]

Oscar's first position in the Cumminsville Turnverein was noted in the *Northside Transcript* of November 27, 1880: "Mr. Edward Herberg, has obtained a lucrative position in a bank down in the city and resigned as secretary of the Cumminsville Turn-Verein. Mr. Otto [Oscar] Sputh takes his place as secretary." Sputh graduated from the Turner Normal College in 1882 and returned to Cincinnati, where he married his fiancée, Anna, on December 14, 1883. Anna's sister, Bertha, was married to William Bruckmann, son of the brewery founder. Oscar worked for free as Turner instructor, but a yearly benefit (always well attended) was held to compensate him for his time. From Cincinnati, Oscar moved to Indianapolis to be instructor for the Indianapolis Turners from 1884 to 1888. He moved back to Cincinnati in 1889 and ultimately moved to Chicago, where he was instructor for the Chicago Voerwarts Turners from 1893 until the 1930s and worked for Chicago public schools.[168]

While in Indianapolis, Oscar testified against August Ries in the Chicago Haymarket trials in October 1886. He told about a mysterious man who came into John Phillip Deleuse's saloon talking about things that were going to happen in Chicago and carrying a heavy satchel, suspected of being a bomb.[169]

Oscar's son, Carl B. Sputh, was a toddler in Cincinnati when his father was instructor for the Cumminsville Turnverein. In the 1930s, Carl served as president of the Turner Normal College in Indianapolis. Collaborating with Indiana University president Herman B. Wells, his term as president ended with the merger of the Normal College and Indiana University in 1941. This became the Indiana University School of Physical Education and Tourism Management. Afterward, Sputh continued his service to the school in an advisory capacity. A scholarship fund was initiated in 1957 to honor his life and service to university.

The Turner legacy of the family continued through Dr. Carl B. Sputh Jr., a graduate of the Indiana University School of Medicine. He continued the family tradition of service to the school, engendering a spirit of goodwill and philanthropy in his five children and his grandchildren. The Sputh family led the effort in 2008 to secure and contribute $50,000 to renovate the Sputh Round House at Turner Camp Brosius. This family legacy and servicc to the American Turner Society all started with Oscar Sputh and the Cumminsville Turnverein.

CUMMINSVILLE TURNER CIVIL WAR VETERANS

Phillip Siebert was born in Hesse-Darmstadt, Germany, and came to America in 1842 with his parents. In 1861, he entered the Fourth Ohio Cavalry, Company E, as a private, lasting until 1864, during which he was taken prisoner at the Battle of Perryville. He started a gardening business in 1872 in Cumminsville and was also a member of the Northside Fishing Club.[170]

Andrew G. Spaeth, also a member of Cumminsville Maennerchor, served in Company C of the Eighty-third Ohio Voluntary Infantry. After the Civil War, he operated an undertaking and funeral parlor business on Spring Grove.[171]

Caspar Tschuss, a founding member, was a cannoneer in Company I, Ohio First Artillery, also called Captain Dilger's "Lederhosen Batterie," and lived at 4041 Spring Grove Avenue. In 1889, he threw a big celebration for the twenty-sixth anniversary of the Battle of Gettysburg in Cumminsville.[172]

Major George Elsasser (1842–1890) was born in Württemberg, Germany, and lived on Kirby Avenue in Cumminsville; he was also a Civil War veteran. He was proprietor of the Dorman House on Spring Grove Avenue, a saloon originally owned by Fred Dorman, a Cincinnati Turner who moved to Cumminsville. Elsasser hosted two hundred men of the Lima, Ohio Turnverein at the Dorman House for the 1889 Cincinnati Turnfest.[173] His son, George F.M. Elsasser, became a District Three Cincinnati police officer.[174]

Wilhelm Sanders, the original founder of the Cumminsville Turners in 1870, was born in Bavaria and enlisted in Company E of the Ninth Ohio Regiment in 1861 when he was eighteen.

When the Israel Ludlow Grand Army of the Republic (GAR) Post took over the old Apple Street Church, the members removed the steeple to mount a cannon that had been captured at the Battle of Pea Ridge in March 1862.

The Cumminsville Turner Maennerchor was a very active portion of the society and was very well known to the larger non-German Cumminsville community. In August 1872, the choir performed a sort of marching/singing serenade from Doerr's Hall on Hoffner Street (near the Turnhall) to Rebel's Hall on Colerain Pike across from Wesleyan Cemetery.

An 1877 article of the *Northside Transcript* brags about how much great music can be heard in the area, "with the fine performances, of course, of the [Turner] Maennerchor." The Turnhall hosted in the 1870s and 1880s very popular choral performances of the children of German language and musical teacher Friedrich Conrad.

This is a lithograph of George Elsasser, Cumminsville Turner, Civil War veteran and proprietor of the Dorman House.

The April 1879 *Northside Transcript* noted that "[t]he German pupils of the public schools of the 25th ward under direction of their teacher, Mr. Conrad, gave an enjoyable entertainment at Turnhall Thursday evening, which was witnessed by one of the largest audiences ever assembled at the hall. The exercises were spirited and showed careful training, the signals of the great crowd of spectators showered them unqualified endorsement of Mr. Conrad and his effort on behalf of the children." The concerts were used as fundraisers to purchase organs that Conrad used at the public schools.

The Cumminsville Turner Maennerchor serenaded members at their weddings and honored them in song at their funerals. The *Northside Transcript* of 1886 has an interesting excerpt: "Gus Schneider, Esq. of Runnymede and Miss Carrie Wehman of Hoffner Street were married last week. They were tendered by an elegant serenade by the Turner Society of which Mr. Schneider is a member."

Cumminsville has long been known for being a mustering place for musicians, artists and those with creative spirits. That legacy was influenced by the Turners. Herman Krumpe, one of the original founders of the Cumminsville Turnverein, was described in this way: "Mr. Herman Krumpe, the well known artist and musician is suffering from a severe throat disease, but it is hoped by his many friends that he will soon be about again."[175]

The Cumminsville Turners were involved in the events of one another's lives, from weddings to funerals. Cumminsville Germans led funeral parades from the houses of the deceased to the Apple Street Church, with bands, singers and large groups marching behind the casket:

> *The funeral of Mrs. John Caspar Bruckman (1832–1889) was one of the largest that has been seen in this ward for many years. She was a member of the Turner Ladies Society and other organizations of Cumminsville. The pall bearers were Messrs. Caleb Dodsworth, August Gulow* [president of the Cumminsville Turners], *John Miller, Henry Dreman, A.M. Streng, and a Mr. Wolf from Cincinnati. The four head officers of the*

> *Turners represented that organization...The funeral procession started from the family residence on Division Street at 2 P.M. and proceeded to the German Protestant Church, on Apple Street, where a beautiful and touching sermon was preached by Reverend* [Christian] *Schenk. The brewery employees and Turners, and the other societies of which she was a member contributed beautiful floral decorations.*[176]

A beautiful excerpt from the *Northside Transcript* of February 10, 1879, shows another instance of how closely knit the Cumminsville Turners were and how active they were in the mourning of their members:

> *Last Monday February 1, the remains of the late Valentine Doensch were buried from the vault at Spring Grove, where they had been placed a few months ago. After prayer by Reverend Henry Miller, Mr. Charles Haebe, President of the Cumminsville Turnverein, delivered a most touching tribute to the memory of the deceased brother, who was a valued member of the above named society. A very beautiful funeral chant was sung by the Turner Maennerchor and the body then committed to the earth. May he rest in peace!*

When the collisions of two trains near Spring Grove Cemetery caused the gruesome death of a former Cumminsville Turner, Charley Keller, a hardware merchant, "The Turners were all represented at the funeral services."[177]

On April 13, 1889, the Turners were present at the funeral of another beloved member, the "Deutsche Apotheke," or German pharmacist, Charles Bristle: "The sad finale to his sickness forseen and dreaded by sorrowing fact and finally occurred. Services were held Thursday afternoon at the German Protestant Church. Reverends Schenk and Anderson officiating. The Turner Society of which he was a member participated in a body, sparing no pains or expense."[178]

Charles Bristle was the founder in 1877 of Bristle Pharmacy at Knowltons Corner at the corner of Hoffner Street and Spring Grove Avenue on a building now occupied by a BP station. After his death, his son, Harry C. Bristle, took over the pharmacy and opened an additional location at the corner of Hamilton and Chase Avenue now occupied by Schaeper Pharmacy. Its motto was "Our drugs are as good as our Sodas." The Bristle sodas were known in Cumminsville to be in a class by themselves.[179]

The Cumminsville Turners disbanded in about 1895. The Panic of 1893, and the building of a new German Evangelical Church on Hoffner

This 1885 photo shows Oscar Sputh, physical instructor for the Cumminsville and North Turners and later the Chicago Turners. *Courtesy of IUPUI.*

Street, had seriously drained the funds of the Cumminsville Turners. The new church would have a large meeting hall, as well as a shooting range in the basement. Those who wanted to be active Turners joined the North Cincinnati Turners in Corryville, only a short streetcar ride away. The hall was then sold to J.W. Streng, who operated it as a boardinghouse and events hall until his death in late 1895. Although the Cumminsville Turners disbanded, they had been instrumental in bringing the Turner principles out of downtown and into the suburbs as the German American migration continued.

The North Cincinnati and West End Turnvereine

Reason against all superstition.
—Turner constitution

By the 1880s, German immigrants and their families were moving up the hills out of the downtown basin for larger spaces and cleaner air. This trend engendered discussion among Cincinnati's hilltop suburbanite Germans to start their own Turnverein closer to their homes. Corryville had experienced rapid population growth before the 1880s, and there was a definite need for a new Turner Society. Corryville sat central to the other Eastern Hill suburbs of downtown Cincinnati like Clifton, Walnut Hills, Mount Auburn, Avondale, Hyde Park and Fulton, all of which were experiencing similar growth. A mural on McMillen Street greets visitors to Cincinnati's neighborhood of Clifton Heights with the German phrase "Wilkommen," indicating the deep German roots of that neighborhood.

Taking advantage of this sentiment, Cincinnati Turner cofounder Gustav Tafel called a meeting on June 19, 1881, at Beuhler's Hall on the corner of Vine and Charleton Street to discuss the formation of a society. The seventy-four men who responded to this call were entertained at that first mass meeting by the Cincinnati Turner Maennerchor. Gustav Tafel was made chairman and Justis Kreuckmeyer secretary. The constitution of the organization was drafted by Charles Joseph, Adolph Krebs and John Finn, all well-respected Cincinnati Turners. The constitution was approved, and the Nord Cincinnati Turnverein (NCTV), or North Cincinnati Turners, was founded on June 26, 1881, with seventy-four members.[180]

A second meeting on June 29 inaugurated the first officers of the organization: Gustav Tafel as president; Emil Heun as vice-president; Franz Neubauer as first Turnwart; D. Koch as second Turnwart; Justus Kreuckmeyer as recording secretary; Louis Kaiser as corresponding secretary; P.V.C. Thilly as treasurer; and Adolph Krebs, Charles Joseph, John Finn, John Correll and Moritz Pohlmann as trustees. In addition to the men's active classes, a number of children began attending classes, adding to the success of the organization.[181]

The organization found a suitable first Turnhall in Beuhler's Hall, quickly procuring gym equipment to start classes. In mid-July 1881, a search for an instructor was begun, and William Stecher was unanimously hired, taking charge on August 2, 1881. In order to spread the word about the new organization, to increase membership and needed funding, a Volksfest was held on October 1, 1881, at the Bellevue House in Mount Auburn, showing off the work of the children's class. A successful 1881 Christmas raffle was held at the Central Turnhall to build funds for a new Turnhall.[182]

From the funds generated at the Christmas raffle, the organization bought a lot at the corner of Vine and Daniels Streets. A small Turnhall was erected on the lot and was opened on November 5, 1882, with a huge dedication ceremony. Turners Carl Joseph and John Krebs Sr. issued bonds to secure funding for the hall and the future of the organization. The opening of the hall increased membership, and soon the organization had some gymnasts among its active members.[183]

Even before the new hall was dedicated, two Turners, George Singer and Franz Kirschner, took first prizes in an Ohio local Turnfest on May 29, 1882. Under the direction of instructor William Stecher, the North Cincinnati Turners carried off first prizes in calisthenics at the national Turnfest in Newark, New Jersey, in 1885.[184]

The word of this new and growing Turner Society caught the ears of the National Turner Organization, and officials were contacted to join the National Turnerbund. However, Second President P.V.C. Thilly advised the organization to remain an independent Turner Society so as not to have unneeded expenses. The Ohio District Turners contacted the society in 1883 to join the district and the National Turnerbund. However, in the spring of 1884, President Thilly passed away, and his successor, Adolph Krebs, advocated their joining the National Turnerbund.[185] So, on June 16, 1884, they became a member of the Nord Amerikanischer Turnerbund

(North American Gymnastics Association) and thus became one of "der drei Liebling," or three young kids, along with the newly formed West End and Lick Run Turnvereine.

With a huge increase in membership, it soon became apparent that they would need to expand their hall, so an addition was added. The organization's fifth anniversary was celebrated in the new hall on August 29, 1886, and the keys were presented to then president J.C. Wagner, with a speech given by Gustav Tafel. By the Cincinnati National Turnfest of 1889, the North Turners had three hundred members. This hall served its purpose for many years, but by the 1890s, it had become clear that another renovation was needed. Tafel and William Ricker were appointed trustees to arrange for the funding, and on November 26, 1893, the magnificent new hall was dedicated.[186]

Architects Anton Rieg and Joseph Marty created an amazing three-story Romanesque masterpiece capped with a north-facing tower, with embedded Turner iconography on the building.[187] The Turnhall housed a bowling alley, preceding the installation of one at the Central Turnhall downtown. The bowling club had several intramural teams who competed—like the Rail Polishers and the Flazamas, a Volunteer Bowling and Minstrel Club and a Regular Bowling Club.[188] A rentable lodge room, a clubroom and a director's room created all of the needed space for this large organization. Members received special Sunday privileges to the clubroom, where many business and political deals were made, much like in the Central Turnhall downtown.

These photos show some of the Turner symbolism present on the North Cincinnati Turnhall. The left photo shows the owl "gargoyle," a Turner symbol of wisdom, on the Vine Street first-floor façade. The right photo shows the emblem of the Cincinnati Turngemeinde on the Daniels Street gym entrance. The owl again appears flanked by the oak leaf wreath, a symbol of victory. The sword symbolizes involvement in the Civil War and preparedness, and the *fackel* (or torch) lights the path to progressive activism.

Above: The *kegel bahnen* (bowling alley) in the North Cincinnati Turnhall, installed before the one at the Central Turnhall on Walnut Street. *Courtesy of Cincinnati Historical Society.*

Below: The North Cincinnati Turnverein's Turnhall in Corryville.

Very generous bondholding members of the organization, along with increase in membership, helped to keep the North Cincinnati Turners financially healthy. By 1906, they were one of the largest Turner organizations in the entire North American Turnerbund, with 1,300 pupils of both sexes.

Nicholas C. Seuss (1872–1928) became the Turner instructor for the North Turners in 1897, and his skill and prowess became pillars of the organization. Seuss, born in Sparneck, Germany, had just graduated from the Turnlehrer Seminar when he was hired. He was the festival instructor for the 1909 Cincinnati Turnfest. The German Turner contingent that came to the United States for the 1905 Turnfest in Indianapolis gave high praise to the organization and members' physical exhibitions and took that acclaim with them back to Germany.

Nicholas Seuss also became famous nationally for inventing the game of kickball, originally called "kick baseball," in 1917. He was then supervisor of Cincinnati Park Playgrounds in addition to being North Cincinnati Turner instructor. The North Cincinnati Turner girls' class organized its own kick baseball league in 1918. In about 1920–21, "kick ball" was used by physical education teachers in public schools to teach young boys and girls the basics of baseball.[189]

Also due to the success of the organization was the Ladies' Auxiliary, always willing to aid when necessary. The NCTV ladies society was founded

Nicholas C. Seuss, physical instructor for the North Cincinnati Turners and inventor of kickball in 1917. *Courtesy of Kevin Grace.*

These are the officers of the NCTV Ladies Auxiliary in 1906. *First row, left to right*: Mrs. George Singer, Mrs. L. Kirstein, Mrs. O. Schroeder, Mrs. Ignacz Grimm and Mrs. W. Ruehl. *Standing, left to right:* Miss N. Esberger, Miss E. Weier and Miss Charlotte Ocker. *Courtesy of Cincinnati Historical Society.*

in 1886 at the home of Mrs. Bauer, who became the first president, along with Mrs. Albin Stecher, husband of the former Cincinnati Central Turner instructor. Other prominent family names involved with the Ladies Society were Mrs. Justis Kruckemeyer, Mrs. Dieterle and Mrs. Seuss. By 1906, the society had three hundred active members, the same number of total organizational members in 1889.[190]

For many years, the North Turners played at the baseball field in Cumminsville at Knowltons Corner under the Ludlow Viaduct, suggesting a connection to the former Cumminsville Turners. Many active members of the North Turners lived in Cumminsville/Northside. The North Turners had indoor and outdoor baseball teams, which competed in intramurals and within the district. Two of the intramural teams were the Corryville Hoboes and the Norwood Bums.

Advancing the notion of mental gymnastics, the NCTV hosted a District Mental Turner Competition at its hall on Sunday, November 29, 1903, with poetry recitation, debate and presentations of papers on Turner topics. Another was held at the hall during the 1909 Cincinnati National Turnfest.

Demonstrating the musical connection of the Turners, on May 12, 1910, the North Turners had a Saengerfest sponsored by Otto Juettner (1865–1922), a noted physician, historian and composer of music, married to Estella, daughter of West End Turner president August H. Bode. Juettner composed a songbook for the Cincinnati Turnfest of 1909 and wrote the alma maters for the University of Cincinnati and Xavier University. The Saengerfest included pieces by Beethoven, Chopin and Rachmaninoff.[191]

North Turners showed their support for the community in many ways. They led the charge to save the Cincinnati Zoo in 1918 by buying five hundred booklets of twenty-five season tickets each. North Turner William H. Lueders led the charge in fundraising for the German Protestant Orphan Asylum in Avondale, raising $21,000 at their 1918 Fall Festival.[192]

WORLD WAR I AND ANTI-GERMAN SENTIMENT

From the time that World War I broke out in Europe in 1914, propaganda flooded the United States. Most of it had a pro-British slant, describing the United States as a "cultural brother." Germany was seen by most Americans as a dangerous monarchy with autocratic militarist thinking, including worries about a hidden agenda to undermine democracy and U.S. power. There were allegations of industrial sabotage, poisoning water supplies, kidnapping individuals and engaging in espionage within American labor unions to keep the United States busy on the homefront. These rumors, along with extensive submarine warfare, added to the distrust of the Germans. Cincinnati German organizations were not immune from this distrust. A new era of nativism began to spread throughout the country.

In reaction to this growing distrust, a special meeting of the North Cincinnati Turners was held on April 4, 1918. At that meeting, a proposition was adopted: "Resolved, that Article I of the Constitution be changed, eliminating, '*The Nord Cincinnati Turn Verein*' and substituting the words, 'North Cincinnati Gymnasium.'"[193] A new sign was quickly added on the front of the Turnhall on Vine Street. A suggestion was even made to anglicize the job of Turnwart, or class instructor.

Their monthly publication, the *Nord Cincinnati Turnleben* (or *North Cincinnati Turner Life*), was renamed in June 1918 to the *North Cincinnati Gym News*. The German Turner motto of "Frish, Frei, Stark, und Treu" was also removed from the front page of this publication.

> *Our boys should bear in mind that this meet* [Ohio Turners District Field Day, June 9, 1918, in Rosedale, Kentucky] *is of special importance, because it will be the first one in which we shall enter under our new name. For more than a generation NCTV has had a most enviable reputation and its athletes and gymnasts always made a good showing at all the Turnfests and in every meet they entered. We must now*

The Turner newsletter *Nord Cincinnati Turnleben* (top) and its name change to *North Cincinnati Gym News* (below) in 1918 to avoid suspicion of connection to Germany.

> *see to it that the name of North Cincinnati Gymnasium shall become equally as famous and just as highly respected, and war or no war, we must prove our superiority over our rivals by cleaning up on June 9 as a starter for NCG.*[194]

The organization rallied to show that it was a patriotic American organization with no ties to the current German regime. By June 1918, Turner Robert Fuerst had raised $50,000 within the North Cincinnati Turner organization in a liberty bond fund drive.[195] Also in June, president Gustav Clemens recommended the formation of a Turner Boy Scout Troop under the leadership of instructor Nic Seuss, Henry Hoefle, Dr. Norton Dock and Carlisle B. Johnston. Playing on its all-American origin, the editor of the *Gym News* said that "no better way has been devised to install into a boy love of nature, discipline, honor, manliness and many other desirable traits, than the Boy Scout Movement."[196]

Earlier that year, North Cincinnati Turner president Gustav Clemens (1861–1932), a Cincinnati public school teacher, suffered persecution and humiliation due to his involvement with the Cincinnati Schlaraffia Society, which was raided by federal officers under suspicion of disloyalty to America. The Schlaraffia Society, which prohibits talk of religion and politics at meetings, is one of the most benign German social organizations in America. Clemens was investigated by the board of education and exonerated of any suspicion. In the *Gym News*, editor Adolf Varrelmann stated: "We consider the incident closed and will try to forget it as one of the many unpleasant and unlooked-for incidents of the war. The silver lining to the dark cloud were the many expressions of confidence and sympathy Mr. Clemens received, among them a letter signed by the children of one of the schools where he instructed."[197]

Gustav's family poured out their support to show their American patriotism. His son, Sergeant Walter Clemens, enlisted, serving for the campaign in France, and Gustav's two daughters went to Washington, D.C., to work for the War Department.[198]

This exodus of enlistees seriously decimated the active classes at the gym during World War I. Many letters from the training camps and the front in Europe were published in the *North Cincinnati Gym News*, all praising the physical training they had received at the North Cincinnati Turner Gym. Those Turners not serving held a tobacco fundraiser stag for the boys in the service on August 18, 1918, at the Newport Elks Camp in Dayton, Kentucky. At the event, a service flag was dedicated with sixty-nine white stars, indicating the number of North Turners serving in World War I, and one gold star, honoring the fallen North Turner Charles Naegelin. Later that year, another North Turner, Sergeant Otto Wiebel, was killed by a German machine gunner near Cuisy in France. A total of seventy-three North Turners served in World War I, and two would not come back.[199]

Statistics released in June 1918 reported that two thousand members of American Turner Societies were serving in World War I in the army or navy. Of those Turners, only 6.8 percent of applicants were rejected for physical unfitness, compared to a much higher 33.0 percent of non-Turner applicants. The *North Cincinnati Gym News* proclaimed, "The large difference undoubtedly proves that regular physical exercise is of great benefit to our young men and enables them to pass the rigid examination for army service easily." It was also reported that 40.0 percent of the Turners enlisted were volunteers rather than draftees.[200] Interesting to note that the drillmaster of the U.S. Army officers in 1918, Major Herman Koehler, was an active Turner and graduate of the Turner Normal College.[201]

At the same time they were fighting German distrust, North Cincinnati Turners and all of the nation's Turners were also actively fighting prohibition. An advertisement from the International Union of United Brewery and Soft Drink Workers in the *Gym News* asked people to "write and speak to your state assemblymen and state senators to work and vote against the ratification of the National Prohibition Amendment to the Constitution." The same *Gym News* complained:

> *The prohibition fanatics are working overtime to put this nation on the blink. Posing as reformers and religious moralists, they are permitted to harass and embarrass every lawmaker with impunity. In this respect, they fully live up to their reputation, and it would be illogical to expect them to listen to reason and use common sense. If they were able to do that there would be no prohibition movement. Personal liberty is one of the first prerequisites of a democracy, but while we are fighting and sacrificing the flower of our manhood for this principle abroad, we are underestimating and misjudging the menace of prohibition to our free institution at home. And while we are fighting for liberty, let us make a clean sweep.*[202]

Unfortunately, the Turner lobbying was not effective in blocking the passage of the Eighteenth Amendment, and from 1920 to 1933, Turner organizations across the country lost organizational revenue from the sale of beer at their halls and social events.

The last physical instructor of the North Turners was Clifford Baum, who participated with the Covington and Central Cincinnati Turners in local exhibitions in the 1920s to help bolster falling Turner membership. Cliff was an active North Turner, helping them win the relay race at the Denver National Turnfest. Baum was a World War I navy veteran and an instructor at the Indiana University School, where his friend and fellow North Turner, Carl Meyer, said, "I am told, he was loved and respected by all his pupils from the smallest girls, of whom he thought so much, to the big, strapping boys on his athletic teams." Meyer continued: "Cliff's sunny disposition would make the Sphinx smile, and we all envied his tremendous strength and athletic prowess."[203]

Prominent Members

Edmund Brendamour Sr. (1859–1931), a longtime member of the Central and North Cincinnati Turnverein, was the founder of the well-known Cincinnati company Brendamour Sporting Goods. Generations of Cincinnati children were sized for soccer cleats or baseball gloves at a neighborhood Brendamour store. Edmund was born and raised in Cincinnati's West End by two Bavarian immigrants, Frank Brendamour (1834–1875) and Susannah Hoffman Brendamour (1834–1909), who operated a successful millinery store on West Sixth Street after her husband's death.

Edmund Brendamour Sr. opened a fancy sports and motorcycle store on Fifth Street in Cincinnati in 1902, near where the Westin Hotel stands today. That store, Roll-Crawford & Brendamour, later moved to Sixth Street and operated into the 1920s. During that time, Edward Brendamour Jr. succeeded his father, formed a new partnership and changed the name to Bolles, Brendamour & Company. His other son, Frank Brendamour, also a Cincinnati Turner, traveled the world and became athletic director for a club in Yokohama, Japan, before World War II. Bolles, Brendamour & Company supplied the award medals for the 1909 Cincinnati Bundesturnfest, as well as gym equipment to all of the Cincinnati and Northern Kentucky Turner Societies. It also sold bicycles, distributed guns for the Hunter Arms Company and supplied uniforms to the Cincinnati Reds during 1908.[204] Bolles, Brendamour & Company was passed to a third generation through grandson E. Jack Brendamour and remained in business until 1997, just shy of one hundred years of providing sports equipment to Greater Cincinnatians.

Edmund Brendamour Sr. competed nationally as a lightweight in Greco-Roman wrestling, defeating in 1884 the undefeated Bernard McFadden in St. Louis. In the late 1880s, Edmund Brendamour Sr. became the first physical instructor for the Cincinnati police force, teaching the officers the benefit of Turner-style free exercising, as well as weightlifting. The *Cincinnati Enquirer* proclaimed, "A number of heavy weights have reduced themselves, so that they now are grand illustrations of what muscular exercise can do."[205] Other Cincinnati Turner instructors, like August Gulow, followed in Brendamour's footsteps as Cincinnati police instructors.

Cincinnati German vernacular architecture was influenced by two Cincinnati Turners. Jacob J. Rueckert was a member of the North Cincinnati Turners, while his older brother, Emil G. Rueckert, was a member of the Central Turners. Both were products of Woodward High

The NCTV active class that competed in the 1885 Newark, New Jersey Turnfest under the direction of William Stecher, son of early Cincinnati Central Turner instructor Albin Stecher. They won first place in Indian club exercises. *Courtesy of the Cincinnati Historical Society.*

School, a Turner-influenced high school, and both were trained as architects at the offices of German architect George W. Rapp, known for his large-scale German brewery commissions. Their commissions were oriented toward the German American community, through connections made at the Turnhall. Jacob tended to have larger brewery commissions, like the Hauck, Moerlein and Windisch-Mulhauser Breweries—all families belonging to the North Cincinnati Turners. Emil tended to have more private residence commissions, although he did have one brewery commission in the Moerlein Brewery in Nashville, Tennessee.[206]

Emil also designed the factory and apartments of the Albert Doscher Candy Company at Jackson and Twelfth Streets in Over-the-Rhine, famous for its Cincinnati favorite, the French Chew, first made in Cincinnati in the 1890s. The Doscher Candy Company also made a caramel corn candy before the invention of Cracker Jack that was sold at the Cincinnati Redlegs' stadium, due to Turner ties to owners of the Reds—the Haucks, Gary Hermann and the Fleischmanns.[207] Harry Doscher, grandson of the candy founder, was an active member of the North Cincinnati Turners.

Anglo-American Speaker of the House Nicholas Longworth III was a member of the North Turners.[208] The historic Longworth family mansion in Hyde Park, Rookwood, was only a short carriage ride from the Corryville Turnhall. In addition to being a very important political connection, after 1894, Longworth gave the North Turners a great tee-time connection to the newly formed Cincinnati Golf Club, carved out of his own estate. Needless to say, his silver-tongued wife, Alice Roosevelt Longworth, was not a member of the North Turner Damenverein.

Another Anglo-American politico, John Benson Foraker, rival of the Longworth political family, was a member of the North Cincinnati Turners, indicating the organization's prominence and the importance of the German vote to local politicians.[209] Foraker had defended the case of John Flora, who claimed to be the illegitimate grandson of Nicholas Longworth I and thus equal heir in the Longworth estate to Nicholas Longworth III and his cousins.

The North Cincinnati Turners boasted as an active gymnast member the famous Rookwood artist Carl Schmidt (1875–1959). Carl, who joined Rookwood in 1896, was known for his scenic plaques and vases featuring landscapes and Venetian marine scenes under velum glazes. Works by Carl Schmidt have repeatedly broken auction records for Rookwood pieces in the past ten years. He left Rookwood in 1927 for the J.F. Johnston Paint Company and then worked for the *Cincinnati Times Star* as an illustrator. He and his wife, Hulda, lived many years at 2815 Euclid Avenue in Clifton.[210]

Wilbur and Orville Wright were presented with certificates of *Ehrenmitglied* (Honorable Membership) on June 3, 1909, by the North Cincinnati Turners. This was a few weeks before the brothers' great homecoming celebration in Dayton, Ohio, and the Cincinnati National Turnfest of 1909.[211] A similar diploma in 1909 was awarded to Frederick Albert Cook (1865–1940), an explorer who claimed to have discovered the North Pole in 1908. These were certainly actions intended to show off their prominence as they hosted the Cincinnati National Turnfest of 1909.

In the 1910s, Turners Henry Hoefle and Edward Simper were proprietors of "the Clifton," the movie theater that became today's Esquire Theatre, located at Telford and Ludlow Avenues in Clifton. During World War I, they mixed advertisements for the North Cincinnati Gymnasium with messages of war propaganda. In 1918, they advertised, "Those Soldier Boys!! Our boys are back on furlough from the training camps—don't they look fine? That's what proper physical culture does—send your children to the North Cincinnati Gymnasium at Vine and Daniels, where they can learn to swim and where they will receive instructions and get the exercise necessary for a sound mind and body."[212]

Julius (1872–1925) and Max (1877–1951) Fleischmann were active members of the North Cincinnati Turnverein.[213] Julius was the elegant dandy, while Max was the tough outdoorsman, traveling the world on expeditions with friends like Teddy Roosevelt, William Boeing and Jimmy Roberts. Max was also a baseball player, an amateur boxer and a superb tennis player. Julius and Max owned the Cincinnati Redlegs in the early 1900s. Both were sons of Silesian Jewish immigrant Charles, and Max transformed the Fleischmann Company into an international giant. Julius was the Republican mayor of Cincinnati from 1900 to1905.

John, Jacob and George Moerlein—sons of Christian Moerlein, founder of the brewery—were active members of the North Turners.[214] The Moerleins were members of the St. Philippus German Evangelical Church located on the northwest corner of McMicken and Ohio Streets, just blocks away from the Moerlein Brewery. The Moerleins donated the large pipe organ to the church, which held services in German until 1921.

Charles and Louis Hauck of the Hauck Brewery were active members in 1906.[215] Their father, brewer John Hauck and a West End Turner, bought the American Association Reds in April 1886 from fellow brewer John Herancourt. Under this ownership, his son Louis devised a set of privileges or "concessions" for $2,100 that a local company purchased to operate food and Hauck beer vending at the stadium.

There were several Turner hangouts in the Corryville and Clifton neighborhoods. Bellevue House was a popular spot for German Cincinnatians and Turners. Mecklenburg's Gardens has been in operation on Highland Avenue in Corryville since 1865. Originally owned and operated by John

The 1906 NCTV Board of Directors. *First row, left to right*: Henry Hoefle, H. Angebrandt, George Singer, Anthoy Eisen, Ernst Goedicke (squatting), Adam Benus, Phillip Finkelheimer and Gustav Lambeck. *Second row, left to right*: Paul Schob, Henry Riechers, Fred Hoffman, Oscar Schroeder, Henry Finke, Henry Franke, Phillip Pfalzgraff and Edmund Brendamour. *Courtesy of Cincinnati Historical Society.*

The presidents of the North Cincinnati Turners from inception to 1903. *Top row, left to right*: Moritz Pohlmann (1884), Theo C. Shubert (1899–1900), George F. Dieterle (1897–99), William Rieker (1891–92) and P.V.C. Thilly (1883). *Middle row*: Emil Heun (1882–83), Ernst von Bargen (1902–3), Gustav Tafel (1881–82; 1892–95), Henry Hoefle (1900–1902) and Adolph Krebs (1884). *Bottom row*: Dr. AH. Klein (1887–88), Jacob Hardung (1890–91), Julius Pfleger (1895–97), Alfred Herholz (1888–90) and Johann C. Wagner (1884–87). Other presidents not included in this photo are Gustave Clemens (1904; 1918), Anthony Eisen (1905) and Wilhelm Lundres (1909). *Courtesy of Linda Houston, Covington Turners.*

Neeb as the Mount Auburn Garden Restaurant and Billiard Saloon, Louis Mecklenburg, an active North Cincinnati Turner[216] who bartended for Neeb, bought the business in 1886. A patron could take the Highland Avenue or Vine-Burnet cars to the door. Carl Mecklenburg, son of Louis and an active member of the North Cincinnati Turners, took over the business from his father and ran it in the 1920s. The Highland House, Imwood Park and Burnett Woods were also hangouts for events, picnics and practice exhibitions for the North Turners.

The North Cincinnati Gymnasium removed itself from the American Turnerbund in 1921 to further distance itself from the distrusted German connection. But local nativism had seriously knocked the wind out of the organization's sails. Membership dropped to an unsustainable level, and the once prominent North Turners had closed their doors by the mid-1930s.

The 1917 North Turners group at Burnett Woods. Mathilde Schmidt (a fifty-year member) is fourth from left in the second row; her sister, Helene, is third from left in the first row. *Courtesy of Peggy Schmidt.*

Cincinnati West End Turnverein

Immigrants flocked to Cincinnati's highly concentrated West End during the next great wave of German immigration after the Civil War. The West End was crowded with pork-packing houses, breweries, wagon works, iron foundries and lumberyards. The West End Turnhall was surrounded by five lumberyards—Wells & Cassidy, James Dunlap & Company, V. Whitney, Taylor & Fulkner and F. Roberts & Company. These lumberyards supported four neighborhood furniture businesses—Still & Duhlmeyer, Betts Street Furniture, F.J. Bennekamp & Brothers and William Becker & Company—as well as the David Gould Carriage Company. Two iron foundries—the Phoenix Iron Works and Knecht & Brown Foundry—were located within six blocks to the east of the West End Turnhall. These enterprises employed thousands of immigrant laborers.

Cincinnati West End's population was even more concentrated than its original German neighborhood of Over-the-Rhine. Originally home to the wealthy, prominent West Enders built sturdy brick homes with gardens at the heads of the sidewalk and stairs leading to an elevated entrance. The Dayton Street Historic District is the last evidence of the once prosperous West End. The district was once known as "Millionaire's Row" and is bounded by Bank Street, Poplar Street, Linn Street and Winchell Avenue.

Many of these new West Enders were Turners in Germany, as well as Cincinnati Turners who moved out of Over-the-Rhine. The trip to the Walnut Street Turnhall became too inconvenient. As a critical mass of these German Turners settled in the West End, it became obvious that a new Turner Society was needed, Cincinnati's fourth Turnverein. So, Cincinnati's West End Turnverein was founded on December 3, 1881, by Henry Boehling and Robert Georgi. Other founders were Richard Ziedler, Louis Rodenburg. Henry Barth, Leopold Kleybolte, Carl Fruehlich, John Tackenberg, August Bode, John Reinhart, Peter P. Brauch, John Roth, Henry Teckel, Friedrich Lackamp, William Retzisch, Robert C. Georgi, Adam Wieger, F.L. Starke, Christian Fritz, Carl Haenle, August Wampach and Friedrich Bone.[217]

Early presidents of the West End Turners were also very connected to the German Republican Club in Cincinnati. Presidents of the West End Turnverein from 1881 to 1889 were Richard Ziedler, August H. Bode, William Retzisch, Robert C. Georgi, Heinrich Boehling and Christian Fritz.[218] Bode was the German Republican Club's president in 1894, with Ziedler its secretary in 1884.

Robert C. Georgi (1846–1907) emigrated from Prussia with his parents to Dayton, Ohio, in 1854. There he was a Zoeglingsverein member of the Dayton Turners in 1858. He served with the 131st Ohio Infantry Regiment during the Civil War and settled in Cincinnati's West End at 915 Dayton Street. He was the West End Turnverein's first secretary and later served as its president. He was also deputy clerk of the United States Court, Southern Ohio District. Being involved with the federal courts for more than thirty-six years, Georgi was said at the time of his death to know more attorneys than any other man in the state.[219]

There were forty members in the first year, but membership had grown to four hundred members by 1883. The large spike in membership necessitated the building of another Turnhall. Children's classes were originally held in a small building on the corner of Liberty and Linn Streets, but this proved to be too small for the growing organization. So, a building committee was formed composed of John Hauck, J. Tackenburg and Henry Behrens, and a building association

This 1889 engraving shows August Heinrich Bode (1843–1918), the second president of the West End Turnverein, serving from 1885 to 1888. He was born in 1845 in Peine, Hanover, where he studied mathematics and engineering. He immigrated to Cincinnati in 1868 and was very active in Cincinnati public schools, writing books about elementary education learning methods.

was established to finance the construction. The cornerstone of the West End Turnhall was laid on April 28, 1883, and construction took three years to finish.[220]

When it was completed on September 16, 1886, the keys were given to then building manager William Retzisch. On September 26, 1886, a large dedication ceremony took place at the hall, and an address was given by President A.H. Bode: "This day is a proud day, Turners and friends. It is forgivable if West End Turners raise their heads in pride to others, with this magnificent new hall, whose banner, flutters in the wind, high above the houses, as a landmark visible miles away. Progress has built a solid castle for the German community!"[221]

The Turnhall was a massive five-story German Romanesque building, with the crest of the West End Turners in the crown point of the roofline. Its street-side windows were tall, with prism glass on top to make the most use of natural light for the gymnasium. The hall housed many great events for the organization. On February 22, 1889, Washington's Birthday, the Turners hosted a masked ball at the hall. On January 26, 1902, a Turner Day for the Ohio Turner District was hosted at the Turnhall.

Some of the physical instructors of the West End Turners were Peter P. Brauch (1889); Friedrich Greimper (1889); Guido Werner (1898–99); and Dr. E.A. Poos (1907–8), who later went on to become physical instructor at Hughes High School in Clifton. Gustav Eckstein came to Cincinnati to serve as the instructor for the West Cincinnati Turnverein in 1889. He later became instructor for the Cincinnati Central Turners.

As with other neighborhood Turner Societies, the West End Turners were connected to local churches, a local brewery and a local park to celebrate

This is a lithograph of the West End Turnhall on Freeman Avenue.

festivals. Two German-speaking churches in the West End area were related to the West End Turners: the German Evangelical St. Marcus Church on Clark near Freeman and the First German Reformed Church on the west side of Freeman Avenue, opposite Findley Street. Only a few blocks from the Turnhall were the large Eleventh District Public School on Clinton Street and St. Mary's Hospital on Betts Street. The Hudepohl Brewery was located in the West End factory district and would have supplied the stock of the Turnhall bar, as well as the many sponsored events.

Lincoln Park, created in 1860, was the West End's only park and Cincinnati's oldest. Only two blocks away from the West End Turnhall on Freeman Avenue and Hopkins Street, it was the favorite spot for the West End Turner picnics and outdoor celebrations. It housed a picturesque lake (for rowing and swimming in the summer and ice skating and hockey in the winter), a wading brook, public baths, a baseball diamond and tennis courts. In the summer, an estimated 1,500 tenement dwellers slept there to escape the stagnant air of their homes. By 1920, the area was a slum and was cleared for the Union Terminal campus. The only remnant of Lincoln Park is the statue of John J. Desmond, a victim of the 1884 Cincinnati Courthouse riot. His statue, which stood atop a large monument in Lincoln Park, now stands in the lobby of the main courthouse downtown.

This 1893 photo shows the North Cincinnati Turnhall Gymnasium, with a group of active Turner members demonstrating various activities. Robert Nohr was instructor then. *Courtesy of the Cincinnati Historical Society*

There were other hangouts for West End Turners. An incline near Freeman Avenue took visitors from the West End basin to the Price Hill House on the top of the hill. People came from all over Cincinnati to ride the incline, dine at the Hill House, enjoy the finest view of Cincinnati, promenade the latest fashions along the boardwalk or catch a glimpse of some other notable visiting the area. But the West End Turners didn't limit themselves to fun in their neighborhood. In 1884, they held a big picnic and Summernight Fest at the Bellevue House in Clifton, another favorite Turner hangout.

Another important landmark in the West End was the original Cincinnati Redlegs Ballpark. In 1884, the park was constructed at the corner of Findlay and Western Avenues and became the home field for the Cincinnati Reds for more than eighty-five years. At first, it was nothing more than a ramshackle grandstand, with players batting into the sun. But several renovations made it into a more elegant ballpark. Its first renovation came in 1894, but then a fire in 1900 made a new grandstand necessary. It was supervised by Central Turner Gary Hermann and christened "the Palace of the Fans." It was renamed Redland Field in 1912 and Crosely Field in 1930s, when inventor Powell Crosley Jr. bought it. Many Turner field days and gymnastics exhibitions were staged there over the years.

The 1893 North Turners' knabenklasse, or boys's class. *Courtesy of the Cincinnati Historical Society.*

The Reds were owned by various Turners. West End Turner John Hauck bought the Reds in 1886 from fellow brewer Herancourt, which had also employed many Turners. Under Hauck's ownership, his son, Louis, devised a set of privileges or "concessions" for $2,100 that a local company would purchase to operate food and Hauck beer vending at the stadium.[222] North Turner Julius Fleischmann and Central Turner Gary Hermann owned the Reds from 1902 to 1927, along with boss George B. Cox.

Other local concession products sold at the Reds' stadium and owned by Cincinnati Turners included Jung, Moerlein, Red Top, Brucks Beer and Doscher's caramel corn. The Rolls-Crawford-Brendamour Company, a North Turner–owned sports accessories business, supplied the Reds' uniforms in 1908.

The last great event that the West End Turners hosted was their silver anniversary in October 1906, with a Jubilee Celebration and local Turnfest attended by the Central and North Cincinnati Turners, as well as Newport and Covington, Kentucky Turners.

Overall, the West End Turners were very active in gymnastics. The peak of membership for the organization occurred in 1883, when it counted a total of four hundred members. They hosted the 1889 Cincinnati National Turnfest in the West End. Membership hovered above the North Cincinnati Turnverein until about 1893, when North Turners surpassed them in membership. After that, the West End Turners experienced a steady decline until they disbanded in 1910. Unfortunately, like the majority of Cincinnati's West End, the Turnhall was demolished to make way for Interstate 75 in a massive urban renewal project.

The Northern Kentucky Turnvereine

Justice from all exploitation.
—Turner constitution

The Newport Turnverein

The Newport Turners were the second local Cincinnati Turner Society formed. Many of the first Central Turners lived across the river in Newport, Kentucky. Because there was no bridge across the Ohio River until the Roebling Suspension bridge was completed in 1867, it became very inconvenient for Newporters to ferry across the river to meetings. Therefore, Wilhelm Pfaender, Heinrich Barth and John Liebert formed the Newport Deutsche Turngemeinde on August 21, 1852, which was incorporated by the Commonwealth of Kentucky on 1856.[223]

The society was organized in a frame cottage bounded by Central Avenue and Liberty, Seventh and Eighth Streets at the farthest west end of Newport. Two years later, a new frame cottage was acquired on Orchard Street. As the only German social club in the city, the society had grown to about seventy members by then. Members and their families met every Sunday evening to practice gymnastics, sing and listen to speakers. The organization was very connected to St. Mark's Lutheran Church.[224]

The population of northern Kentucky at the time was composed primarily of slaveholding members of the Whig and Know-Nothing Parties, and the Germans faced much nativism. Determined to carry on their physical and mental training, the Newport Turners survived this nativist period and won respect in the community. As with other local Turner organizations, Newport quickly formed children's classes for boys and girls. It was in the Newport Turnhall on Orchard Street where the Turners of Cincinnati, Covington and Newport held off the Anglo-Kentuckians in the *Pfingstmontag* Riot of 1856.[225]

A Ladies Society was formed in 1858, and like other societies, the members made a flag for the organization. They helped to fund the expansion of the Orchard Street hall by staging Newport's first theatrical performance, a play called *Love's Dream* by the Newport Turner Theatrical Society. In addition to the theatrical society, the Newport Maennerchor society was received into the Newport Turners in June 1879. The organization hosted minstrel shows in the 1910s at its hall. Many other events, such as masked balls, suppers, raffles, picnics and entertainment of various kinds, were held throughout the season to support the organization, all with help from the Ladies Society.[226]

During the St. Louis Turnfest of 1861, the Newport and Covington Turners shared an instructor who unfortunately disappeared with the society's funds, putting it into severe debt. Many Newport Turners answered President Lincoln's call and joined the Ninth Ohio Regiment to preserve the Union. Because of this, activities of the society practically ceased until after the Civil War.

At least one of the Newport Turners played a part in the building of the Roebling Suspension bridge. Heinrich Steinhauser immigrated to Newport, Kentucky, from Germany with his daughter. He learned his profession of stonemasonry while working on the bridge. He was part of the group of northern Kentucky Turners that traveled to settle New Ulm, as well as one of the lucky who survived the Indian attack in 1862.

The society's Golden Jubilee was celebrated on June 29, 1902, with a Turnfest including the Dayton, Cincinnati and Covington Turners at the Queen City Race Track. Other big events at this time were the annual May Day celebrations at Spink's grounds on Linden Avenue, where more than 1,200 children participated in folk dances, games and sports. They also hosted a Mental Tournament on Sunday, April 17, 1904, with readings of essays on "Advantages of Immigration to the United States," poetry recitation and debate on topics such as "Does War Further Civilization?" and "Should the Miami and Erie Canal Be Reconstructed and Improved?"[227]

In 1907, the Newport Turners notified the state board of education and lobbied to make physical education part of the Kentucky public school system. They promoted education by sponsoring scholarships for students in the Newport School System.[228]

By the turn of the century, the Orchard Street hall had been outgrown, and a new gymnasium and hall was completed in 1912 on Sixth Street, corresponding with a successful funding and membership bazaar. It housed a gymnasium and swimming pool. Like other Cincinnati Turner Societies, Newport members shared their instructor with the local high school. David Reese led the Newport High School basketball team to the championship in 1915.[229]

World War I had an effect on the Newport Turner Society. Fifty Newport Turners enlisted or were drafted into service, and membership dropped. Instructor Ben Wiley conducted a military training class in the gym that greatly assisted in preparing the boys for service. It was at this time as well that the society name was changed from Newport Deutsche Turngemeinde to the Newport Gymnastic Association, due to the fear of association with anything German.[230]

William K. Streit came to the Newport Turners in 1921 as instructor, staying until 1927. He turned the organization around, leaving it with the highest member roll in its history. In his farewell address, he said that upon seeing the decrepit state of the gymnasium when he arrived in June 1921, he had almost turned around and walked out. Streit produced a monthly newsletter for the organization, *The Gymnast*, from 1921 until he left in 1927.[231]

The organization continued on after Streit left, sponsoring physical education reviews and pageants at its gym. Turner Circuses were held in the 1930s, with Rockette-like shows. The society hosted a Boxing Show on October 25, 1931, as well as moonlight cruises on the *Island Queen* steamboat for fundraising activities.

In 1927, Newport Turners hosted a Diamond Jubilee Pageant to celebrate their seventy-fifth anniversary: Boys Day was held on May 7, at Fort Thomas, Kentucky; Girls Day was on May 14, at Newport City Park; a historical pageant was held on May 18, at Bellevue Ball Park; an anniversary banquet took place on May 19 at the Turnhall; and a Turnfest and picnic were held on June 5, at Cold Spring, Kentucky.[232]

The first amateur boxing tournament ever held in northern Kentucky was staged at the Newport Turnhall on November 18 and 25, 1931, sanctioned by the Amateur Athletic Union and by the Kentucky State Boxing Commission. There were nine divisions, ranging from special weight to heavyweight. The Newport Turners entered about twenty boys and had entries from Blue Grass, Silver Grove, Fenwich and Friars Athletic Clubs and the Central YMCA, as well as from several others. Newport Turner boxing instructor Otto Technow directed the tournament, and Clifford D. Schneider, state boxing commissioner, supervised.[233]

This 1902 photo ("A Group of Old Timers") features longtime Newport Turnverein members.

Then, in February 1932, near the end of the Prohibition era, beer was found during a raid on the Newport Turnhall. The case went to trial, and the president, Emil Krauss, was dismissed in court on the grounds that the beverage confiscated was never analyzed.[234] At this time, Newport had a nightclub and gambling scene similar to Las Vegas, Nevada. Having local judges who were sympathetic to drinking helped the case's dismissal.

Instructor Streit had saved the organization after World War I. But after he left in 1927, the organization continually lost membership until it disbanded in 1936. The effects of economy, anti-German sentiment and loss of revenue from beer sales during prohibition took a toll on Greater Cincinnati's second-oldest Turnverein.

The Covington Turnverein

Liberty and progress are given as the reasons for the founding of the Covington Turnverein on September 13, 1855. The Know-Nothing movement was at its climax, and anti-German nativism was pandemic in northern Kentucky. Men of strong character and courage were needed to oppose this discrimination. These brave men who founded the organization were John Heltemes and Gustav Mauer, saloonkeepers; Dr. Schwartz, a physician; Carl Bettman and John Friedland, soap manufacturers; Wilhelm Adam, a wagon manufacturer; Arnold Fricke, a tailor; Bernard Weymeyer, a bookkeeper; and Gottlieb Bruestle, a beer driver. At least 110 members joined in 1855. A committee quickly formed to draft a constitution for the organization. But when the liberal nature of the original constitution was presented, only 40 of the 110 original members stayed. The constitution took a firm stance against slavery, agreed to vote for no political candidate who was a member of the Know-Nothing Party and declared to oppose all prohibition laws as unconstitutional.[235]

In 1857, John Geisbauer purchased a small lot for the first Turnhall on Pike Street, near where the Pike Street Chesapeake and Ohio Railroad trestle stands today. The property had an exercise area, a saloon and rooms to lease. The good location in the central business district gave them good rental income to help fund the organization. To prepare for any further nativist attacks, strict rules were laid down by the organization in 1860 requiring mandatory attendance at sharpshooting practice for members. The *Pfingsmontag* Riots in 1856 had made them hypervigilant for further attacks.[236]

During the Civil War, the organization was decimated; by the end of the war, only seven Turners remained. The Turnhall was sold to Xavier Seidel, who built a new hall in front and moved the Turners to the back, allowing them to keep their furniture, piano and songbooks and remain in the old hall. In 1865, they moved to a third property, called the Rising Sun, and grew with new immigrants from Germany who sympathized with their movement. A Zoeglingsverein (children's class) was formed in 1865 that, in 1873, was expanded with a drawing class. Gustav Tafel, General Willich and Dr. Blau lectured on scientific and political topics before the Turner forum.[237]

In 1868, they moved to Workingman's Hall, temporarily, and bought the property on Pike and Ninth Streets, which would become their fourth home. It was dedicated on April 30, 1870, with great fanfare attended by the district societies extant at the time—Cincinnati, Cumminsville and Newport.

In May 1877, an agreement was reached with Turner Gottlieb Bruestle to purchase his property at Pike and Main Streets for their fifth and final home. On May 10, a cornerstone-laying ceremony took place, with large fanfare, and the new hall was dedicated on October 1, 1877. In 1890, young ladies' classes were added to the organization, and in 1898, a Singing Society was founded. A tornado on July 7, 1915, ripped the roof off the Turnhall and caused the collapse of the balcony and the destruction of all of the windows, but they were repaired. A pool would be added in the lot next to the hall in 1913. During the 1937 flood, the hall was used by the Red Cross as a refuge for displaced victims, with home-cooked meals by the Ladies' Auxiliary.[238]

The Covington Turners suffered a second round of anti-German sentiment during the world wars. The use of the German language was discontinued at the Turner meetings in 1915. The group changed its name from Turngemeinde to Covington Turners Society in 1918, and some Germanic-sounding street names were rechristened. Riedlin Avenue, named after the longtime Covington Turner president and owner of Bavarian Brewery, became Pershing Street. Despite the resurgence of anti-German sentiment, twenty-four Covington Turners served in World War I, and thirty-two served in World War II.[239] From 1915 to 1921, the organization had its own newsletter, the *Turner Echo*, edited by Alban Wolff Sr.

In 1919, after the passing of the Volstead Act to enforce prohibition, a significant portion of Turner revenue and socialization was repressed. However, home-brew was produced by many of the German immigrant members, and parties continued to be held at the Turnhall. A letter drafted in 1932 from the Covington Turners congratulated Kentucky congressman Brent Spence (1874–1967) on his stand against prohibition in the U.S. House of Representatives.[240]

The organization was closely tied to St. Paul's German Evangelical Church in Covington. Riedlin, Roth and owners of Lewisburg brewery were also members. Minstrel shows were staged at Mother of God auditorium, a Catholic parish in the neighborhood that had the largest stage.

The Covington Bears were formed on October 8, 1899, and Henry Rauch was its first *oberbear*. A unique arrangement lasted until the outbreak of World War I: all bears in the Ohio District received a standing invitation to appear every New Year's Day at the Covington Turnhall for an open house. Sometimes up to 150 bears gathered at the gym and, after exercising, had great fun at a real old-time *Commerz*.[241]

The Bear Den was where older Turners congregated to "stick their schnozzle into Red Top Honey [beer]," and it was equipped with a buzzer

Above: The members of the1902 bear class of the Covington Turners pose humorously in their gymnasium.

Below: The Covington Turner active class whose members competed in the 1897 national Turnfest in St. Louis, Missouri. They proudly display their winning wreath, still framed at the Turnhall today. *Courtesy of Linda Houston, Covington Turners.*

Top: The ladies' class of 1900–1901 was under the instruction of George F. Roth. Positioned in front of them are the dumbbells and Indian clubs they used in their exercises.

Bottom: The men's active class of 1905, under the instruction of Henry Weber.

so that younger Turners could serve them. Although now a game room, the Bear Den is lined wall to wall with the organization's awards and is memorialized to Louis Leucht, a fifty-year member with the Covington Turners.

William Riedlin (1851–1919), an active Covington Turner, served several terms as president and was the owner of the Bavarian Brewery, just a few blocks south of the Covington Turnhall. Born in Baden, Germany, he immigrated in 1868 to Cincinnati, where from 1878 to 1882 he ran Tivoli Beer Garden on Vine Street. In 1882, he moved to Covington, Kentucky, and bought Myers Brewery, transforming it into the Bavarian Brewery enterprise. He was an active member of Covington Turner Bears and a competitor in national and district competitions. He served for several years as president

William Riedlin, shown here in 1888, served as president of the Covington Turners and the Ohio Turner District and was owner of the Bavarian Brewery.

of the Ohio Turner District. He and his son, William Jr., were victims of the 1919 influenza epidemic.[242]

One famous building in Covington was built by a Covington Turner president and owned by another Covington Turner president. The Hermes Building, now Molly Malone's Irish Pub at Fourth and Court Streets, was built about 1888 by Joseph Hermes (1835–1918) as a saloon called the Covington and Newport Exchange and Arbeitershalle (Workingman's Hall). Joseph Hermes immigrated to the United States in 1853 and was elected as a Democrat to the Kentucky legislature in 1872. He became a judge and was elected as Covington Turner president from 1880 to 1881. While in the legislature, he opposed the purchase of Bibles for representatives, prayer at the opening session and use of the legislature hall for the convention of a temperance organization called the Good Templars. He was also president of the German American Mutual Protection Association of Covington, the main purpose of which was to abolish Sunday liquor laws. As a saloonkeeper, Hermes was once indicted by a grand jury for serving liquor to a minor, but the case ended in a hung jury.[243]

In 1926, Covington Turner president Alban Wolff (1890–1949) bought the Hermes Building for his printing business. Four large offset lithography presses in the basement and on the first floor ran twelve hours per day.[244]

As with other Turner organizations, the physical instructor was a very important position in Covington. Henry Weber served as gymnastic instructor from 1898 to 1914. From 1914 to 1930, the gymnastic instructors who served came in this order: Al Whole, Al Landwehr, Carl Varrelmann, Carl Duning and William Bischoff. Carl Varrelmann was the son of North Turner president Adolph Varrelmann and had just graduated from the Turner Normal College before serving his one year. In August 1930, Louis A. Roth was elected as director of gymnastics, a position he held until 1972. Class enrollment was at its peak in 1930, with 207 pupils enrolled. Gym instructors who followed after Roth were Eleanor Risch, former Central

Covington Turner president Alban Wolff and the Hermes Building, where he ran his printing business.

Turner instructor Jeannine Schilling, Paul Ankenbauer, Gay Trame, Joyce Baker and Katie Wesseling.[245]

Louis A. Roth (1906–2002) came from a third-generation Covington Turner family. He taught gymnastics and dance with his wife, Mutzie Wolff Roth, at the Covington Turner Society for forty-two years. His parents, Louis Sr. and Betty Roth, were also active Covington Turners. Louis A. Roth taught at Bloom Junior High School, to which he rode his bike five miles one way each day to work. He and his wife worked with the children at Devou Park Orphanage and were members of the St. Paul Evangelical Church. When he retired in 1972, he was awarded the American Turner Hall of Fame Award. He was also awarded the *Bund der Getreuen* (Order of the Faithful) by the National Turnerbund for membership of more than forty years and participation in at least four national Turnfests.[246]

During the late 1930s, softball and volleyball became popular. Men's and women's volleyball teams did well in regional and national competitions. The board continued to upgrade the athletic facilities with new shower rooms, restrooms and lockers to retain good membership.

In 1944, Turner George Steinford was given permission to use the Turnhall as the Poor Children's Christmas headquarters. Under Steinford's leadership, this society gave new and reconditioned toys for underprivileged children in northern Kentucky for many years.[247]

Turners faced great change in the 1950s after World War II. Membership dropped as Covington residents moved to newer suburbs.

Louis A. Roth was the longest-serving physical instructor for the Covington Turners, from 1930 to 1972.

Women were accepted as full members in 1950, which helped to bolster membership. The Women's Auxiliary stepped in to host various fundraisers, which were able to finance outstanding debt and delinquent taxes. A one-hundred-year anniversary of the organization was celebrated in 1955 with great fanfare.[248]

During the 1960s and 1970s, the Turners sponsored both basketball and knothole baseball teams for youth. In 1967, a youth club was established, breathing new life into the society. Men's basketball flourished from the early 1960s into the 1980s. From this group has come the core leadership for the last fifty years. Golf and softball also attracted and retained membership in the Covington Turners.

This hall stands today in the still very German Lewisburg neighborhood of Covington. Behind the Turnhall is Glier's, the world's largest goetta manufacturing facility; the large campus of the Bavarian Brewery; and a plethora of century-old German church spires. The fact that the Covington Turners still exist in their 1877 facility can be attributed to the opportunities provided for members that can't be found elsewhere. The society still encourages its members to hold divergent opinions, often discussed over a beer at the Turnhall bar. As much true in 1855 as in 2011, the bar is the ideal forum for expressing controversial ideas and experiencing *gemütlichkeit*.

Dayton, Kentucky Turnverein

The Dayton, Kentucky Germans banded together on Sunday, April 22, 1877, at John Moeller's Hall with fifty members.[249] Dayton, Kentucky, was only a few miles east and downriver from Newport, Kentucky. The first president of the organization was Charles Laible, the first physical instructor was Victor Schneider and the treasurer was John Moeller, the owner of the hall.[250] On December 8, 1877, they hosted an exhibition by Dayton public school students as a fundraiser for their school bell.[251] They celebrated a first-year anniversary in December 1878 with delegates from the Cumminsville, Newport, Covington and Cincinnati Turner Societies coming and sent delegates to the National Turner Convention in 1884; however, they folded into Newport and became inactive shortly thereafter.[252]

A Falmouth, Kentucky Turnverein existed in 1873. Covington Turners attended a picnic that they hosted that year with their band, surely encouraging them to join the district.[253] A Lexington, Kentucky Turner organization existed as early as 1859 and into at least the 1890s.

Other Small Cincinnati Turnvereine

Free speech, free press, free assembly for the discrimination of all questions.
—Turner constitution

Dayton, Ohio Turnverein

Dayton, Ohio, was the fourth southwest Ohio Turnverein to be founded when ten German Americans came together on March 18, 1853. Similar to Cincinnati, Dayton had a wealth of breweries and industries that employed a sizeable German immigrant community. With the arrival of the Cincinnati, Hamilton and Dayton Railroad in the 1850s, the Turner communities of these three cities were easily linked. As a result, there were many family connections between the Dayton Turners and the various Cincinnati Turner Societies. Two country suburbs of Dayton with German populations had short-lived Turner Societies. Piqua to the north and Miamisburg, Ohio, to the south both had societies from the late 1850s up to the Civil War.

The first Dayton Turner officers were John Bittmann, president; Ignatz Szabo, vice-president; Charles Theodore Tisch, secretary; A. Junkermann, first instructor; Heinrich Lorenz, instructor; and Johann P. Dietz, Jacob Loeb, A. Tylle, Charles Engel, Rupert Russ and A. Fehrmann, trustees.[254]

The first Turnhall was known as French Town School House, located on Montgomery Street. It was purchased in 1861 from the Dayton Board of Education and used until 1877, when the current Turnhall was purchased.[255]

Above, left: The current Dayton Liederkranz Turnhall on Fifth Street, with a service star flag indicating the number of Dayton Turners serving in World War I. *Courtesy of Dayton Liederkranz Turners.*

Above, right: Fred Olt, longtime Dayton Turner president and president of the Ohio Local District. *Courtesy of Dayton Liederkranz Turners.*

Like the Cincinnati Turnvereine, the Dayton Turners were closely tied to their local brewery, the Olt Brewery, which incorporated in 1907. Through prohibition, it made soft drink brands Vita Cream, Superba and Olt's Orange and polar distilled water, as well as distributed dairy products. When the Olt Brewery closed in 1949, its operation was sold to Cumminsville Turner–owned Bruckmann Brewery. Many members were also members of the St. John's Lutheran Church.

John N. Olt (1840–1921), a Bavarian immigrant, incorporated with his five sons: Charles (1866–1940), Fred (1874–1958), Edward (1885–1918), Oscar (1884–1964) and William (1865–1912). John and all of his sons except Charles were longtime Dayton Turners—Fred joined in 1893, William in 1895, Edward in 1900 and Oscar in 1902. Following the Turner philosophy, the Olt Brewery funded a public swimming pool on McGee Street near the brewery.[256]

John Olt's wife was Philippina Linxweiler, sister of Jacob Linxweiler Jr., mayor of Dayton, Ohio, from 1896 to 1898. Linxweiler was also an influential member and officer in the Dayton Turngemeinde, joining in 1862. His sons, George, Edmund and Arno Linxweiler, were members from the 1890s to the 1920s.[257]

The Dayton Turners were very active in the Ohio District and hosted a variety of local and district Turnfests in Dayton. They hosted a tri-state regional Turnfest in August 1883. Thousands converged on July 4, 1903, on the city fairgrounds, where the Dayton Turners hosted in fourteen large tents, with hundreds of gymnasts from cities across Ohio, Kentucky and Indiana. Delegates to the Turnfest paraded through downtown Dayton in the morning, and drill teams two hundred strong performed at the fairgrounds using American flags.[258]

A Dayton Ladies' Auxiliary was organized on March 18, 1913, but the ladies had been active with the Turners as early as July 1854, when they presented the society's first flag. The seat of the national Turner Damenverein for many years was headquartered in Dayton under the leadership of Laura Olt, wife of Fred Olt.[259]

The active class of the Dayton Turngemeinde, which competed at the 1889 Cincinnati National Turnfest. The instructor was William J. Herzog. He served without pay from 1887 to 1897, distinguishing the Dayton Turners in many Turnfests, including the 1890 and 1895 Columbus District, 1891 Indianapolis Circuit, 1892 Lima District, 1894 Milwaukee Charity Circus, 1896 Covington District and the 1897 St. Louis National Turnfests. *Courtesy of Dayton Liederkranz Turners.*

The modern Dayton Liederkranz Turner women's choir. *Courtesy of Dayton Liederkranz Turners.*

The Dayton Turners were very active up until World War II. In December 1952, due to sinking membership and finances, a vote was passed to merge the Dayton Turners with the Dayton Liederkranz, which had formed in 1890 as a Singing Society.[260] The Liederkranz moved into the Dayton Turners building on Fifth Street. The widows of the Turner Damenverein used to play cards in the hall and were the last remnants of the Dayton Turners.

Today, the Dayton Liederkranz Turner Society is Dayton's oldest surviving German organization, with a mission to promote the cultivation, furtherance and maintenance of German song, dance, customs, culture and language, good fellowship and participation in civic affairs. The most popular events of the organization are their spring, fall and Christmas concerts by their men's, women's and children's choruses, all of which participate in district and national Saengerfests.

The Hamilton Turnverein

The Hamilton Turnverein was founded as the third southwest Ohio Turnverein in 1852, the same year as Newport, Kentucky. In 1855, they were known as the Turners of Hamilton and Rossville and bought the Hamilton Academy building as their Turnhall, in which they had a library and a reading room. One year later, they ran behind in their payments, and the academy directors were also displeased at seeing their former building used as "a drinking house," in their words. They were willing for the Turners to continue their library but laid down the law about drinking in the building.

Disliking prohibition, the Hamilton Turners refused, and they released their claim on the building. It was sold to Black, Long and Allstatter for a machine shop. By 1861, Turners were meeting every first Saturday evening in Sohn's Hall at 58 Front Street in Hamilton. Fred Wehrman was speaker; John Decker, a Civil War veteran and shoemaker/pension agent, was second speaker; Peter Gaetz was recording secretary; and August Benninghofen and Peter Rieff were librarians. John W. Sohn, father-in-law of William Margedant, was superintendent of the Turner Sunday School, and William was the physical instructor.[261]

The Hamilton Turners were active in the Ohio District until the 1890s, but there is no record of them hosting a District Turnfest or having the local district headquartered in their city. It seems that the German Turners of Hamilton split off into other groups earlier than their Cincinnati-area brethren.

The Lick Run Turnverein

Lick Run was a small community of Germanic immigrants located west of the Mill Creek and downtown Cincinnati. The Lick Run stream flowed down this valley, three miles west of Cincinnati, into Mill Creek. It was not far from Cincinnati's West End, but like in Cumminsville, it offered a path downtown for the community with the feel of the country. Lick Run also had its own opportunities for work. Lick Run was home to two breweries, the Bullock's Curled Hair Factory and ample hillside for gardening and grape growing.

Cincinnati's father of wine and viticulture, Nicholas Longworth I, imported German immigrants to grow grapes for his Sparkling Catawba wine. He owned land in the hills of Lick Run that he rented to these German immigrants. In 1850, Longworth said the following about the area: "Lick Run in our immediate vicinity will make one of the most beautiful rural spots in the world. It will soon be a continuous line of vineyards. I wish some of our poets would visit it in May or June, and give it a more beautiful and appropriate name. They may rack their brains for months, and not find one worthy of the scene."[262]

A Cincinnati Westwood traction line was completed in 1877, traversing the Lick Run hillside and linking travelers from downtown to Westwood. The line was largely financed by Procter & Gamble cofounder James N. Gamble to try to make the west Cincinnati suburbs more attractive to downtowners.

The Lick Run Turner Society was a short-lived Greater Cincinnati Turner Society. The club was founded on November 22, 1881, and was part of the National Association from 1884 to 1889. The president and physical instructor of the Lick Run Turners was Gottlieb Mueller, a teacher in the Cincinnati Public School System. Mueller gave an address at the Central Turnhall when the Lick Run Turners were initiated into the Ohio Turnbezirk. Their first group event was hosting an Ohio Turner Organization meeting at their Turnhall in 1884.[263]

This 1875 building on Montrose Street in Lick Run is believed to have been used as the Lick Run Turnhall.

This is the Martini Evangelical Church, of which many of the Lick Run Turners were members. This photo shows the original small frame church building farther up the hill, built in 1855, as well as the newer 1891 building in the foreground. The Westwood traction line ran in between these two buildings. *Courtesy of Gary Lind.*

The Lick Run Turnhall was a large brick German Romanesque structure that had been built in 1875 into the hillside of Montrose Street. Housing a bowling alley at one time, the basement served as an icehouse for the residents of Lick Run and supplied the several local breweries and saloons.

Like other neighborhood Turner groups, the Lick Run Turners were closely tied to their local church, the Martini Evangelical Church. Most of the members were also members of the Martini Church and are buried in the church cemetery. The most probable reason for the club's disbanding in 1889 was to direct tight funds into raising money to build a new church, which they finished in 1891.[264]

Gottlieb Richter (1831–1909), another Lick Run Turner, came to Cincinnati in 1851 from Württemberg, Germany, and lived at 862 Queen City Avenue on the corner of Williams in Lick Run. He was president of St. Martini Evangelical Church from 1878 to 1888 and also member of the German jaegers or sharpshooters, the Good Fellows Lodge and the German

Butcher's club. Richter Avenue, leading up the hill from old Queen City Avenue to the Martini Church, is named for him.[265]

The Lick Run Turners were also connected to their local tavern. Lick Run had the William Hoffmeister Brewery on White Street at Montrose Street from 1857 until 1871, when Hoffmeister opened a tavern and icehouse at the same location. William F. Hoffmeister (1827–1902) was a Forty-eighter, immigrating to Cincinnati from Ludwigsburg, Württemberg, Germany—the same home city as the three original founders of the Cincinnati Turners. He and his wife, Anna Margaretha (1835–1922), were lifelong members of the Martini German Evangelical Church in Lick Run and had thirteen children. It is possible that William Hoffmeister was a relative of fellow Ludwigsburg immigrant and Cincinnati Turner founder August Hoffmeister.[266]

THE NORWOOD TURNVEREIN

The Norwood Turnverein was the last offshoot Turner Society formed in Cincinnati and can be considered a grandson organization of the original Cincinnati Central Turners because many of its members were first members of the North Cincinnati Turnverein, whose early members were in turn first members of the Central Turners. Although the organization lasted longer than the Cumminsville, Lick Run and West End Turnvereine, it is lost to history outside of the American Turner records. Its history serves a unique purpose in helping to understand the migration of Turner Societies with the second- and third-generation German Americans in Cincinnati.

Norwood was a suburb farther out than Hill Top that became very prominent from the 1910s to the 1930s and, like the West End, was home to some of Cincinnati's wealthiest German Americans in the 1880s. After the formation of the Cincinnati Hill Top Suburbs, wealthy German Cincinnatians moved farther out of the city and formed the affluent village of Norwood, which to this day has never been annexed by Cincinnati, even though it is surrounded by the city. Many North Cincinnati Turners lived in Norwood, and as a convenience, a group of them decided to form their own Turnverein.

The Norwood Turners formed in 1905 with sixty-three members. Their membership peak was sixty-five members in 1907. During the years 1914–22, they reported fewer than eight members each year. Most of the members being of draft and service age probably went off to war. During 1923–26, they renamed themselves the Turnverein Jahn and saw a small resurgence in membership, hovering at about twenty members. After struggling with fewer than eight members after 1926, they disbanded in 1938.[267]

Their first district activity was participation in the Golden Jubilee Turnfest of the Covington Turners at the Covington Ball Park on September 17, 1905, with Cincinnati Central Turners, West Turners, North Turners, Dayton Turners, Findlay Turners and Louisville, Newport and Indianapolis South Side and Social Turners.[268]

August Eckel was the physical instructor from 1907 to 1914. Eckel immigrated to the United States in 1887 from Rheinpfalz, Germany, and met and married his wife in New York, where he was a teacher of physical culture in 1900, according to the U.S. Census. He was a graduate of the Turner Normal College and director of physical training for all Norwood public schools. Eckel, like other Turner instructors, gave much of his time after class hours for directing the athletic teams of the Norwood High School. The Norwood Turnverein is listed in the National Turner records as being headquartered at Eckel's house at 3925 Regent Avenue.[269] Although the Norwood Turners never had their own Turnhall, they probably used the gymnasiums at the various Norwood schools and parks for their exercises and gymnastics practice. August's last position in the Norwood Public School System before retiring in the 1930s was as a teacher at Williams Avenue Public School, one block from his family home.

For the Eckels, Turnerism was a family affair. August's wife, Susan C. Eckel, was also a teacher of physical education at Norwood public schools from 1909 into the mid-1930s, after her husband had retired. Their daughter, Louise Eckel, became a public school teacher, and their son, August John, became a teacher in the city schools of Richmond, Indiana.

August Eckel formed the Norwood High School football team in 1907, the same year the Norwood Turners joined the Ohio District and the National Turnerbund. The season ended with a record of four wins, two losses and one tie. August's son, August Eckel Jr., was quarterback for the undefeated team in 1912. Following the Turner philosophy that sports did not exempt athletes from participating in all-body exercising, the Norwood football program became strong and achieved some amazing records. The team was undefeated in 1910 and again in 1912, when they piled up a score of 180 points to 0 against their opponents during regular season play. Even though their team weight averaged only 135 pounds, they were Cincinnati champions in 1915 and again in 1921, as well as champions of southern Ohio in 1916. This speaks to the effectiveness of the Turner exercise regimen.[270]

This is a photo of the undefeated 1912 Norwood High School football team, coached by Turner instructor August Eckel, with his son, August Jr., as quarterback and Frank "Swede" Sorenson, another star player.

This is a photo of the 1917 Norwood High School swim team. August Eckel, Norwood Turner instructor, is far left, and Edmund Brendamour Jr. is third from the left. *Courtesy of Michael Brendamour.*

Two great Turner football all-stars came out of Norwood. Halfback Frank "Swede" Sorensen became captain of the Ohio State football team in Columbus, Ohio, when they won their first championship in the Western Conference in 1916. So it can be said that Ohio State's football powerhouse legacy was initiated by the Norwood Turners. "Teddy" Leonar Baehr, a Norwood football team graduate of 1914, went on to become one of the greatest fullbacks in the University of Cincinnati football program.[271]

The Norwood High School football team played other Turner-instructed and Turner-influenced Cincinnati high schools, like Woodward, Hughes and Walnut Hills, led by former Central Turner instructor Dr. Alfred A. Knock. Other teams that varied on the schedule were Covington, Hamilton, the Ohio Military Institute and McGuffy High School of Oxford, Ohio.[272]

By 1938, when the Norwood Turners disbanded, those Turner organizations that made it had weathered the Great Depression and the anti-German sentiment of World War I. But now Turner Societies were competing with mass exodus to the suburbs and the many other gymnastic and sports associations available to youth in Greater Cincinnati and northern Kentucky.

The Cincinnati Turners and Their Legacy in Public Education

Mens sana in corpore sano.
—current motto of the American Turners, meaning "Sound mind in a sound body"

The greatest legacy that the Turners left was their influence on the American educational system. In Cincinnati, this Turner influence on public education was significant. Central Turner Henry H. Fick became supervisor of German for Cincinnati public schools in 1903. It was under Fick that the Cincinnati Public School System became nationally known for its bilingual education system.[273] In Cincinnati, many Turners were part of the 180 teachers employed by the board of education in 1909 and decades prior to teach German. In district grade schools that year, 12,585 students (3,096 in the upper grades and almost 1,000 in high schools) were enrolled in German. No other city in America could boast such numbers.[274] West End Turner August H. Bode wrote seven German readers that were used in Cincinnati public schools.[275] But the Cincinnati Turner influence in public education didn't end with German language instruction.

Cincinnati's Turnverein led the nation with the introduction of physical education into the public school system. In 1857, the Cincinnati Turners funded the installation of gym equipment—parallel bars, horizontal ladders and circular swings—at four schools in the German districts of the city. These German districts were the First District on Franklin Street, the Sixth District on Elm, the Eleventh on Elm Street and the Thirteenth on Findlay. Woodward High School at that time also had gymnastic equipment installed. In 1860, Cincinnati Turner instructor Louis Graeser was appointed superintendent of gymnastics for the Cincinnati Board of Education, a position that he held for the next fourteen years.[276]

This is a lithograph of Louis Graeser, Central Turner physical instructor from 1860 to 1873 and first superintendent of physical culture for Cincinnati public schools. *Courtesy of Cincinnati Central Turners.*

The physical instruction was given mainly in the classroom, consisting of calisthenics, dumbbells and ring exercises. Instruction was given by special teachers every three weeks and repeated daily by the class teachers.

Graeser's position was abolished in 1873 due to the financial panic of the same year. He had immigrated to America in 1848, coming to Cincinnati in 1852. In 1855, he left to become instructor for the Milwaukee Turnverein but came back in 1859 to become instructor for the Cincinnati Turnverein. After his forced retirement in 1873 from the Cincinnati Public School System, he organized the prominent Graeser Dancing Academy at the Ohio Mechanics Institute, on the site of today's Emery Apartments.[277]

After 1873, the rules for the practice of gymnastics remained in force in Cincinnati public schools, but without a superintendent to oversee the subject, physical education became neglected. From 1883 to 1887, gymnastics were not officially recognized or taught. But William A Stecher—instructor at the North Cincinnati Turnverein and son of Central Turner instructor Albin Stecher—as well as his successor, Oscar Sputh, both taught unofficially and without pay at the Normal School and the Sixteenth and Twenty-third Districts, respectively. Because of their selfless work, the Cincinnati Board of Education, on May 31, 1887, adopted a rule that allowed students five minutes for calisthenics and physical exercise at the end of each class.[278]

At the Turner National Convention of 1880 in Indianapolis, Dr. H.M. Starkloff of St. Louis, Missouri, proposed a question: "How would it be if we would work with all our might to introduce physical training into the public schools of this country? We could not conceive a more beautiful gift than this to bestow upon the American people. This should prove a worthy enterprise, for whosoever had conquered the youth has gained the future."

This convention passed a resolution calling on its members to work for the introduction of physical education into the curriculum of the nation's public school systems. The Turners took up the issue with enthusiasm and enjoyed many successes over the next twenty years. In addition to work already done in Cincinnati, Chicago, Cleveland, Denver, Indianapolis, Kansas City, Milwaukee and St. Louis were among the cities where Turners' lobbying helped convince school boards to add physical education classes.[279]

During the 1891–92 school year, the four Cincinnati Turner organizations—Central, West, North and Cumminsville, totaling more than one thousand members—elected a joint committee to bring physical education back to Cincinnati schools. Central Turner Alfred Herholz was named secretary for the introduction of physical culture into the common schools. He sent a letter to the Cincinnati Board of Education on November 2, 1891, saying that "the members of the four Turnvereins, or Gymnasia of this city, desirous of having the physical well-being of our youth cared for, as well as the intellectual one, wish to impress upon your honorable body the necessity of a rational physical training of the pupils of our common schools." The Turner organizations offered their three physical instructors to the public schools free of charge, and they were assigned as follows: Gustav Eckstein (West End Turners) was assigned to the Fourteenth and Twenty-seventh Districts, Arthur A. Knock (Central Turners) was assigned to the Sixteenth District and Vine Street School and Adolph Speidel (North Turners) was assigned to the Twenty-third and Thirtieth Districts. After three months of instruction, the board of education accepted this as part of regular schoolwork.[280]

At the same time, Ohio Turners were active during the winter of 1891–92. During the session of the Ohio General Assembly, Sandusky Turner and state representative John J. Molter (1854–1934) introduced a bill providing for the teaching of physical exercise in the schools of certain cities.[281] Molter was born in Sandusky, Ohio, to Baden immigrant Forty-eighter parents and was an active member of the Sandusky Turners, earning a swimming champion title during a competition in Covington, Kentucky, in 1887. He also served as mayor of Sandusky from 1901 to 1910. He was a fan of hiking, which he did every day, even in inclement weather.[282]

On April 13, 1892, a law was passed by the Ohio General Assembly requiring physical culture, including calisthenics, be included and regularly taught in Ohio public schools. The Cincinnati Board of Education, in accordance with this law, adopted a rule providing for a superintendent of physical culture with four assistants. Carl Ziegler of Cleveland, a Central

Turner, was made superintendent in September 1892, and his assistants were Adelaide Spills; Guido Werner, former physical instructor for the West End Turners; Eckhardt Keller, Ohio Turner district physical instructor; and Jacob Rettich.[283]

Dr. Carl Ziegler (1859–1935), a Central Turner and president of the Ohio District, was director of physical education in the Cincinnati Public School System from 1892 until he retired in 1929. Born in Homburg, Germany, he immigrated with his parents to America in 1866. Before coming to Cincinnati, he was physical instructor for the St. Joseph, Missouri Turnverein and the Cleveland, Ohio Socialer Turnverein and also taught at the Chautauqua Summer School of Physical Education from 1890 to 1897. An 1886 graduate of the Turner Normal College, he also graduated from the Cincinnati College of Medicine in 1896. During his term with Cincinnati public schools, his staff grew from four assistants to a corps of ninety assistants who worked under a Turner-lobbied state law requiring one hundred minutes of physical education per week for each child.[284] He wrote a series of four manuals titled *Manuals of Exercise in Physical Training* that was used by the Cincinnati Public School System, and in 1918, he wrote a series of lessons in the *Cincinnati Times Star* for those men of draft age who wanted to get fit for service but didn't belong to a gym.[285]

Covington Turner president Alban Wolff was secretary of the executive board of the German American Alliance of Kentucky and a Kentucky representative. He presented to the state legislature a resolution urging the introduction of physical culture in the public schools of Kentucky to "help prepare our boys for War."[286]

Gus Bachman (born 1866) was a Newport Turner fencing instructor from 1886 to 1888 and a Newport Turner gym instructor from 1909 to 1917 and from 1919 to 1921. During that time, he introduced physical training into the public schools of Newport, instructing classes without pay. After leaving Newport Turners, he was called to lead physical training for Dayton, Kentucky public schools, with the provision that elementary school teachers also had to take physical courses to administer to their children. Born in Cincinnati, he developed pneumonia at the age of five and was advised by a physician to begin taking classes at the Cincinnati Turnverein, then under Albin Stecher's guidance. He competed as an active Cincinnati Central Turner at the Newark, New Jersey Bundesturnfest of 1885. In 1889, he led the Lexington Turners in the Cincinnati Bundesturnfest and the 1893 Milwaukee Bundesturnfest, where his Lexington Turners participated in a Turner Exhibition in the livestock pavilion at the Chicago World's Fair.[287]

Being advocates of early childhood education and activity, the Cincinnati Turners hosted German kindergartens at the North, West End and Central Turnhalls. The free kindergarten movement in Cincinnati was spearheaded by William Authenreith, who had been in the first Cincinnati Turner Zoeglingsverein in 1854.[288] Fostering the child from a young age was considered very liberal in antebellum and even Victorian America, where children were to be seen and not heard. In the Progressive Era, Cincinnati Turners recognized that between the ages of six and sixteen was the time of greatest physical development and the proper time for corrective training.[289]

The Cincinnati Turners made a broad-based cultural education possible to children from the lower and middle classes who wouldn't have otherwise been able to afford a private school education. They received education on literature, music, art, theater and politics. From well-educated physical instructors, the young men were given a noble philosophy of life. The Ladies' Auxiliary or Turnschwestern organizations conducted sewing schools and needlework classes in addition to physical fitness classes for girls and women, and they also instilled in them the Turner principles.

BUILDING A SOUND BODY

The Cincinnati Turners based their fitness programs on Jahn's system of Turner fitness training based on three groups—elective exercises, obligatory class gymnastics and games. Elective exercises allowed a Turner to perfect himself in exercises for which he was physically best equipped, such as running, jumping, vaulting, climbing, swimming or fencing. Obligatory class gymnastics were sets of free exercises and light apparatus work in which every Turner participated for complete body fitness. Finally, the importance of games was recognized for developing alertness, quick judgment, rapidity and decision-making. The Turners understood the need for "play" to keep a free mind throughout a Turner's life from childhood into adulthood.[290]

As competitive team sports were taking off in America at the height of the Progressive Era in the 1910s, the Turners were quick to point out the dangers of one-sport training. A 1918 article in the *North Cincinnati Gym News* presents an early advocation of the modern concept of cross-training: "The War has proven the superiority of the Turners' system of physical culture over modern athletics in a most positive way. One-sided exercise does more harm than good; overtraining actually lowers the vitality of the athlete and shortens his life." By 1918, the Turner system of gymnastics was conducted at the Military Academy at West Point and Annapolis.[291]

Pessimists within the Cincinnati Turner organization in the 1910s argued that with the introduction of physical fitness in the public schools of so many cities, the Turnerbund had outlived its usefulness. However, statistics from World War I and II showed the Turners still outperformed their service mates in physical fitness tests even *with* physical fitness integrated into the public school system.

A diagram of Turner exercises with batons, a group exercise common at Turnfests. Figures 16 and 17 show amazing similarity to the Eastern yoga poses "Salutation" (Anjaneyasana) and "Warrior" (Virabhadrasana), respectively.

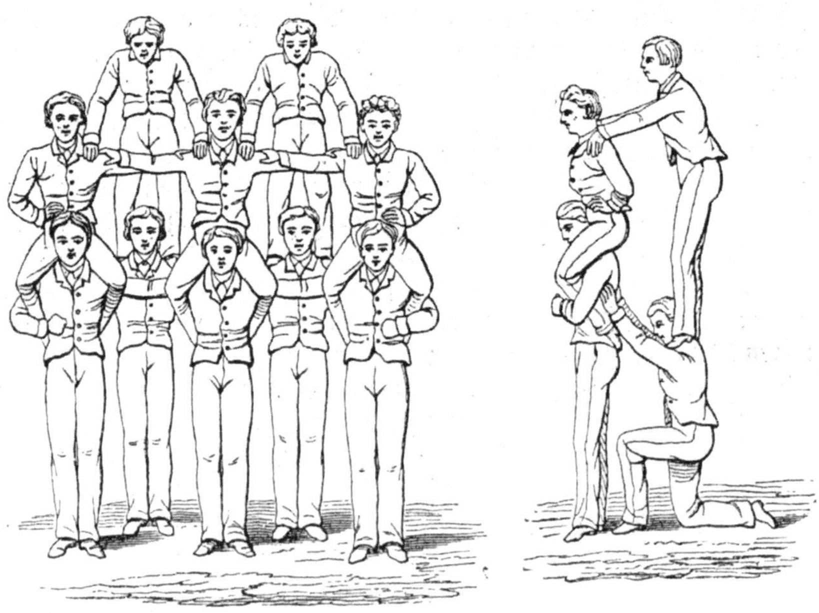

Fig. 31.

Diagrams from a Cincinnati Central Turner library instruction book entitled *Turnerische Gesellschaftsubungen* (*Turner Group Exercises*), printed in Leipzig, Germany, in 1881. They show group acrobatics that Turners showcased at their Turnfests. Note the similarities with modern cheerleading and drill team exercises, which the Turners also influenced. *Courtesy of Cincinnati Central Turners.*

The Turner concept of whole body fitness is very similar to Eastern philosophies like yoga, where every part of the body is exercised to achieve alignment. The Turner form of free exercises, or poses, is very similar to yoga asanas (groups of poses in succession). Excerpts from the library of Turner training books of the Cincinnati Turners show a striking resemblance to forms of yoga.

The job of Turnwart was one of the most important jobs in the Turner organization. The very first instructor for the Cincinnati Turners in 1848 was Carl Leopold Fettweis. He was followed by Louis Wielert, Bernard Froehlich and Adolph Riedel in the 1850s and then Louis Graeser from 1860 to 1873.[292] Instructors were often recruited from other cities' Turnvereine, and the position was usually a launching pad into a lucrative career in the public school system or even at a police or fire department. In the early years, it was not always a paid position, but in some cases the Turner organization had yearly benefits to give instructors a nice sum. Since Turners were connected to the local public school systems in both physical education and German instruction, serving as a Turner instructor could lead to other positions in the public schools. There was even a headhunter for gym teachers in the early 1900s that advertised in *Mind and Body*, which guaranteed finding higher pay for physical instructors.

With the job came great responsibility. The physical instructor was responsible for increasing interest and membership in the organization through public exhibitions, educating the public of Turner ideals and promoting growth of auxiliary organizations like hiking, swimming and bowling clubs. Each Cincinnati Turner instructor left a legacy with the public school system of Cincinnati.

Albin Stecher (1833–1922) was instructor for the Cincinnati Turners from 1873 to 1880.[293] He was also a regimental musician for the Ninth Ohio Regiment in the Civil War from July 22, 1861, to September 10, 1862. His son, Wilhelm Albin Stecher, graduated from the Turnlehrer Seminar in Milwaukee in 1881 after leaving his position at Central Turners. The Stecher family had moved to Calhoun Street in Clifton by the 1890s and joined the North Turners. Wilhelm Stecher wrote more than ten illustrated handbooks on German American gymnastics and children's exercises for grades first through high school, becoming the most prolific American Turner author on gymnastics.

Albin Stecher, Cincinnati Central physical instructor from 1873 to 1880. *Courtesy of Indiana University–Purdue University Indianapolis (IUPUI).*

Carl John Kroh (1852–1937) was born in Baltimore, Maryland, and was a graduate of the Turnlehrer Seminar in Milwaukee in 1879. He was a Dayton Turner instructor from 1879 to 1880, eventually becoming a Cincinnati Turner instructor, where he introduced the annual exhibitions at Music Hall. He was the technical leader of the 1889 Turnfest in Cincinnati, introducing society competition and mass drills for the first time. He left Cincinnati in 1890 to join the faculty of Cook County Normal School in Chicago and was succeeded by Dr. A.A. Knock. Kroh was dean of the Turner Normal College from 1906 to 1911

An older Carl John Kroh, Cincinnati Central Turner instructor from 1880 to 1890.

and supervisor of physical training in Louisville from 1911 to 1915, retiring to San Francisco, California.[294]

Dr. Arthur Alexander Knock (1866–1949), born in Estonia, was Central Turner instructor from 1890 to 1895 and was known as a fine disciplinarian and apparatus instructor. As a child, he had painful chest contractions, and one of his legs was two inches shorter than the other. Through exercise, he corrected these problems. He migrated in 1888 to Napa Valley, California, where he was gymnastics instructor, and then graduated from the Turner Normal College in 1890, heading to Cincinnati. He left as Cincinnati Turner instructor in 1895 to become physical director at Walnut Hills High School from 1895 to 1934 but was an active Central Turner member for more than fifty years, from 1890 to 1948. Knock designed the Walnut Hills Gym in 1903, which looked much like the Central Turnhall, with pommel horses, hanging rings and parallel bars. He also became physical instructor at the University of Cincinnati for five years.[295]

Dr. Robert Nohr was physical instructor for the North Cincinnati Turnverein for four years and succeeded Knock in 1895 as assistant physical instructor to Dr. Ziegler in the Cincinnati public schools. Nohr resigned that position in 1899 to complete his medical studies at the Cincinnati College of Medicine and Surgery, also graduating that year. Nohr had taught physical instruction in public schools and U.S. Turnvereine. Born in Dayton, Ohio, he was a *zoeglings* Turner as a child and an 1890 Turner Normal School graduate. He taught at Louisville Turngemeinde and taught physical culture in Dayton, Ohio public schools; the Trenton, New Jersey Turnverein; and at Fort Wayne and Indiana public schools. He wrote *In the Gymnasium* and was also editor of *Mind and Body*, a monthly journal devoted to physical education. He taught in the Cincinnati Public School System from 1895 to 1899 and from 1908 to 1935.[296]

This 1896 photo of the Walnut Hills gym class shows Dr. Arthur A. Knock, director of physical education at Walnut Hills for more than thirty years. *Courtesy of Jenny French, Walnut Hills Alumni Association.*

Following the Turner legacy, Robert Nohr's son, Paul, was physical instructor and baseball coach at Western Hills High School. "Pappy" Nohr, as he was known, coached a young Pete Rose at Western Hills and described him as "a good baseball player, but not a Brinkman." Edwin Albert Brinkman was a teammate of Rose's and became a major-league shortstop but did not achieve the same fame as Rose.[297]

The three former Cincinnati Turner instructors—Dr. Knock, Dr. E.A. Poos and Dr. Nohr—were all honored in their seventies by *Turner Topics* magazine in 1937 for their influence developing sound bodies for thousands of boys and girls in Cincinnati for more than fifty years each.[298]

Dr. Gustav Eckstein succeeded Dr. Knock as Central Turner instructor from 1895 to 1924 but before that had served as West End Turner instructor. He also served as the physical instructor for the Ohio District in 1898. Born in Falkenstein, Germany, he immigrated to America in 1881 and was a classmate of Dr. Ziegler's at the Turner Normal School. Under his leadership, the Central Turners participated in the national Turnfests at

The Technical Committee for the 1909 Cincinnati Turnfest, made up of instructors from all of the city's Turner Clubs and high schools. *First row, left to right*: August Eckel, Norwood Turners and High School; William Taube, Norwood Public Schools; and Guido Werner, West End Turrners. *Second row, left to right*: Dr. Robert Nohr, Cincinnati Public Schools/ former North Turner instructor; Carl Ziegler, Cincinnati Turners/Cincinnati Public Schools; and Dr. A.E. Poos, West End instructor/Woodward and Hughes High School. *Third row, left to right*: Dr. A.A. Knock, Cincinnati/Walnut Hills High School; Fritz Reuter, Cincinnati Ninth Ward teacher; and Dr. Jacob Rettich, athletic instructor at Woodward High School. *Courtesy of Kevin Grace.*

St. Louis in 1897, Philadelphia in 1901, Indianapolis in 1905, Cincinnati in 1909, Denver in 1913 and Chicago in 1921, returning decorated with honors. He was well known for the beautiful exhibitions at Music Hall under his direction. He was the gym teacher at Hughes High School in Clifton in 1899 when he decided to enter the Ohio Dental College, graduating in 1904.[299] Eckstein practiced dentistry at his home in Mariemont until his death at age ninety-two.

Rudolph L. Memmel, son of a Turner family, took Beyer's place as Central Turner instructor in 1937. He was twenty-five years old, a recent graduate of the Turner Normal College in Indianapolis, Indiana, and had

Above, left: Like many Turner instructors, Gustav Eckstein was a graduate of the Turner Normal College under Charles Brosius in Milwaukee, Wisconsin. This is an early photo from the 1890s. *Courtesy of Cincinnati Central Turners*.

Above, right: Gym Director William P. Beyer, who was Cincinnati Central Turner instructor from 1925 to 1936 and was instrumental in creating a program enabling children from inner-city schools to attend classes for free. *Courtesy of Cincinnati Central Turners.*

been instructor for the Indianapolis Turners, instructor at the Headley Rural School in Bloomington, Indiana, and Turner and swimming instructor in Rochester, New York. He left briefly from 1940 to 1945 for military service in World War II and then returned to his post at Central Turners, taking Cincinnati to compete at the 1948 St. Louis National Turnfest.

During World War II, Henry Zing of Madison, Wisconsin, became instructor and took the Turners to the 1941 Springfield, Massachusetts Turnfest. Robert Ploetz from Sheboygan, Wisconsin, took over as physical director in 1942 until he was called into military service. Then Cincinnati's first female physical instructor, Miss Elinor Risch, took over and kept up classes during the war, until both Ploetz and Memmel returned from the war. Both jointly instructed the Central Turners, but both ended up leaving to become physical directors in the Cincinnati Public School System. Miss Risch again took over, until the Central Turnhall was sold in 1959 and the

Turners moved to their current location at Pinney Lane. She then became physical instructor for the Covington Turners.[300]

Since the move to Pinney Lane, there have not been physical instructors in the same sense as at Central Turnhall on Walnut Street. Without a gym at the new location, the focus of the Central Turners became intramural sports and recreation. So the succeeding athletic director, Don Royer, organized in 1978 intramural baseball, volleyball, bowling, fishing, golf leagues and other sports activities for members. But the legacy left by the Cincinnati Turner instructors is long lasting. Every time a Cincinnati-area student plays kickball or takes a physical fitness test in gym class, they can thank the long line of German American Cincinnati Turners who instilled the values of physical fitness in our American public school system.

Notes

Chapter 1

1. *Cincinnati Freie Presse*, 1885.
2. American Family Tree of Friedrich Ludwig Jahn, www.gymmedia.de.
3. Friedrich Hecker Papers, 1825–1987, Western Historical Manuscript Collection, University of Missouri–St. Louis, introduction, 2.
4. Ibid.
5. Ibid.
6. Ibid.
7. George Eisen and David Kenneth Wiggins, *Ethnicity and Sport in North American History and Culture* (Westport, CT: Greenwood Press, 1994), 21.
8. Ibid., 22.
9. Max Burgheim, *Cincinnati im Wort und Bild* (Cincinnati, OH: M&R Burgheim Printers, 1888), 153.
10. *Cincinnati Volksblatt*, October 23, 1848.
11. Ibid.
12. Burgheim, *Cincinnati im Wort und Bild*, 153.
13. *Cincinnati Volksblatt*, October 24, 1848.
14. Burgheim, *Cincinnati im Wort und Bild*, 153–54.
15. Ibid., 154.
16. Cincinnati Central Turner Records, Turner membership records, 1848–61, Ruth Lily Special Collections and Archives, University Library, Purdue University, Indianapolis, Indiana.

17. Alfred Kierschner, *Historical Journal: A Souvenir of the Centennial Celebration of the New York Turnverein* (New York: Allied Printing, 1950), 12.
18. Eisen and Wiggins, *Ethnicity and Sport*, 20.
19. Friedrich Hecker Papers, 2–3.
20. Burgheim, *Cincinnati im Wort und Bild*, 294–96.
21. Ibid., 154–55.
22. Heinrich Metzner, *Jahrbücher der Deutsch-Amerikanische Turnerei* (New York: self-published, 1890–94), 55.
23. Heinrich Bornstein, *Memoirs of a Nobody: The Missouri Years of an Austrian Radical (1849–1866)*, trans. Steven Rowan (St. Louis: Missouri Historical Society Press, 1997), 153.
24. Susan L. Piepke, *Mathilde Franziska Anneke: The Works of a German-American Activist* (New York: Peter Lang Publishing, Inc., 2006), 72–73.
25. *Indianapolis Turnverein Seventy-fifth Anniversary* (Indianapolis, Indiana, 1926), 8.
26. Ibid., 14.
27. Daniel J. Kenny, *Kenny's Illustrated Guide to Cincinnati* (Cincinnati, OH: R.J. Clarke, 1893), 96–97.
28. *American Turner Topics* (November 1948): 3.
29. Pauline Authenreith Tafel, *Aus Meinen Leben* (Newport, Kentucky, 1907), a memoir.
30. Ibid.
31. Ibid.
32. *Century of Health: American Turners Thirty-seventh National Festival Souvenir Program* (St. Louis, Missouri, 1948), 89.
33. Thomas B. Rentschler, *The Rifles and Blades of the German-American Militia and the Civil War* (Hamilton, OH: Blue Hills Press, 2003).
34. *American Turner Topics* (November 1948): 3.
35. Heinrich Metzner, *History of the American Turners* (Louisville, KY: National Council of the American Turners, 1898), 54.
36. Burgheim, *Cincinnati im Wort und Bild*, 577–79.
37. Clifford Neal Smith, *German American Genealogical Research Monograph, Number 20, Early 19th Century German Settlers in Ohio* (McNeal, AZ: Westland Publications, 1984).
38. Cincinnati Central Turner Records, Meeting Minutes, 1848–61.
39. Carl E. Wolffradt and Benno Damus, *Cincinnati Turnfest-führer. Festschrift hrsg. mit Autorisation des Fest-Committees für das 25. Bundes-Turnfest des nord-amerikanischen Turnerbundes, abgehalten in Cincinnati vom 21–26, Juni 1889* (Cincinnati, OH: M&R Burgheim, 1889), 176, 178.

40. Burgheim, *Cincinnati im Wort und Bild*, 552.
41. Wolffradt and Damus, *Turnfest-führer*, 182.
42. *American Turner Topics*, "Cincinnati Central Turners" (November 1948): 3.
43. Heinrich Metzner, *Jahrbücher der Deutsch-Amerikanische Turnerei*, "Die Tage vom 2. Bis 4. April 1855 in Cincinnati," 1890–94, 5.
44. Heinrich Metzner, *Jahrbücher der Deutsch-Amerikanische Turnerei*, "Die Feier des 4. Juli in Columbus, Ohio," 1855, 90.
45. *New York Times*, July 6, 1855.
46. Covington Turners, *Diamond Jubilee Souvenir Book* (Covington, KY: Wolf Publishing, 1930), 5, 7, 9, 11.
47. Smith, *German American Genealogical Research*, 82.
48. Dieter Cunz, "Egg Harbor City, New Germany in New Jersey," *Report of the Society for the History of the Germans in Maryland* 29 (1956): 9–30.
49. Kenny, *Kenny's Illustrated Guide*, 96–97.
50. Mary Sayre Haverstock, *Artisits in Ohio, 1787–1900: A Biographical Dictionary* (Kent, OH: Kent State University Press, 2000), 287–88.
51. Burgheim, *Cincinnati im Wort und Bild*, 497–98.
52. Metzner, *Jahrbücher der Deutsch-Amerikanische Turnerei*, 39.
53. Walnut Hills Cemetery Records, Carl Sprandel, Section 6, Lot 1119.
54. Burgheim, *Cincinnati im Wort und Bild*, 514–15.
55. Smith, *German American Genealogical Research*, 82.
56. Metzner, *Jahrbücher der Deutsch-Amerikanische Turnerei*, 131.
57. Records of Leavenworth Turners, microfilm roll, Kansas City Historical Society.
58. Alfred Emory Lee, *History of the City of Columbus*, vol. 2 (Columbus, OH: Munsell and Company, n.d.), 772.
59. Metzner, *Jahrbücher der Deutsch-Amerikanische Turnerei*, 125–27.
60. Kremena Spengler, "The Pfaenders: Revolutionaries, Artists, Pioneers—and a Major Pop Star," *New Ulm Journal*, October 12, 2008.

CHAPTER 2

61. *Ohio History: The Scholarly Journal of the Ohio Historical Society* 72 (n.d.): 125.
62. Metzner, *Jahrbücher der Deutsch-Amerikanische Turnerei*, 98.
63. *Cincinnati Daily Gazette*, July 3, 1860.
64. Constantine Grebner, *We Were the Ninth*, trans. Frederic Trautmann (Kent, OH: Kent State University Press, 1987), 4.
65. Ibid., 6–7.

66. Joseph R. Reinhart, *A German Hurrah* (Kent, OH: Kent State University Press, 2010), 1.
67. Grebner, *We Were the Ninth*, 14.
68. Ibid., 48.
69. Ibid., xiii.
70. Honorable Bert S. Bartlow, *Centennial History of Butler County Ohio* (Hamilton, OH: B.F. Bowen and Company, 1905), 866–67.
71. Reinhart, *A German Hurrah*, 277.
72. Grebner, *We Were the Ninth*, 199.
73. Ibid., 54.
74. Reinhart, *A German Hurrah*, 213.
75. Ibid., 209.
76. Ibid.
77. Ibid., 208.
78. Associated Press, "Historian Hunts for Missing Confederate Flags," October 4, 2009.
79. Rentschler, *Rifles and Blades*, 107.
80. Reinhart, *German Hurrah*, 246.
81. Grebner, *We Were the Ninth*, 97.
82. Reinhart, *German Hurrah*, 47.
83. Ibid., 42.
84. Ibid., 97.
85. Ibid., 76.
86. Ibid., 82.
87. Ibid., 237.
88. Ibid., 86.
89. Grebner, *We Were the Ninth*, 150.
90. Ibid., 248.
91. Ibid., 178–79.
92. Ibid., 188.
93. 1898 Roster of Grand Army of the Republic, Cincinnati Historical Society.
94. Ibid.
95. Burgheim, *Cincinnati im Wort und Bild*, 157.
96. Metzner, *Jahrbücher der Deutsch-Amerikanische Turnerei*, 139–44.
97. Grebner, *We Were the Ninth*, 30.
98. Ibid., 193.
99. Ibid., 194.
100. Ibid., 2.

Chapter 3

101. Wolffradt and Damus, *Turnfest-führer*, 173–75.
102. Metzner, *Jahrbücher der Deutsch-Amerikanische Turnerei*, 135.
103. Covington Turner Society, *The First Hundred Years: 1855–1955* (Covington, KY: Wolff Standard Publishing, 1955), 18.
104. Metzner, *Jahrbücher der Deutsch-Amerikanische Turnerei*, 112.
105. Ibid., 252–54.
106. Ibid., 282.
107. Ibid., 150.
108. *New York Times*, 1873.
109. *New York Times*, 1880.
110. *Cincinnati Volksblatt*, June 22, 1889, 10.
111. Ibid.
112. Kevin Grace, *Sporting Man: Garry Hermann and the 1909 Cincinnati Turnfest* (Cincinnati, OH: University of Cincinnati Press, 2004), 10–11.
113. Ibid., 1.

Chapter 4

114. *American Turners Thirty-ninth Quadrennial National Festival, June 29–July 3, 1955* (Milwaukee, Wisconsin, 1955), 37.
115. Arthur Dobling, *Newport Gymnastic Association, Diamond Jubilee Pageant Depicting the History of Physical Education* (Newport, KY: Allied Printing, 1927), 19.
116. Metzner, *History of the American Turners*, 20.
117. American Turner Records, National Council Reports, 1850–60, Ruth Lily Special Collections and Archives, University Library, Purdue University, Indianapolis, Indiana.
118. Metzner, *Jahrbücher der Deutsch-Amerikanische Turnerei*, 212.
119. American Turner Records, National Council Reports, 1880–1900, Ruth Lily Special Collections and Archives, University Library, Purdue University, Indianapolis, Indiana.
120. *North Cincinnati Turner Leben* 3, no. 12 (October 1917): 3.
121. Timothy J. Holian, *Over the Barrel* (Cincinnati, OH: Sudhaus Press, 2001).
122. *Cincinnati Enquirer*, May 2–3, 1886.
123. *New York Times*, June 1876.

124. Friedrich Hecker Papers, Box 2, Folder 20, Item 1 (Lincoln), and Box 3, Folder 33 (Hayes), Western Historical Manuscript Collection, University of Missouri–St. Louis.
125. Gary Hermann Papers, National Baseball Hall of Fame Library, Cooperstown, New York, introduction, 1.
126. Ibid.
127. *Cincinnati Freie Presse*, December 1883.
128. Burgheim, *Cincinnati im Wort und Bild*, 455–56.
129. Ibid., 557.
130. Ibid., 513.
131. *Cincinnati Turner Newsletter*, Cincinnati, Ohio, 1928.
132. Ohio District Turners, *A Symposium of Papers Dealing with Turner Activities* (Cincinnati, Ohio, 1928), 1–24.
133. *North Cincinnati Turner Leben* 4, no. 3 (January 1918): 10.
134. *American Turner Topics* (1954).
135. Dobling, *Diamond Jubilee Pageant*, 45.
136. *Official Minutes of the Thirty-fourth Convention of the American Turnerbund, June 28–30, 1933* (Milwaukee, Wisconsin), 20.
137. *American Turners Thirty-ninth Quadrennial National Festival*, 38.
138. *Cincinnati Central Turners, Sesquicentennial Celebration, August 1, 1998* (Cincinnati, Ohio), 23.

Chapter 5

139. *Cincinnati Volksblatt*, June 22, 1889, 11.
140. Ibid.
141. *Cincinnati Volksfreund*, November 12, 1872.
142. *Cincinnati Volksblatt*, June 22, 1889, 11.
143. Peter Cozzens, *This Terrible Sound: The Battle of Chickamauga* (Champaign: University of Illinois Press, 1996), 290.
144. *Northside Transcript*, 1879.
145. Hugo Gollmer, *Namenlisten der Pioneere des Nord-Amerikanische Turnerbundes der Jahre 1848–1862* (St. Louis, Missouri, June 1885), 22.
146. *Souvenir History of Cumminsville* (Cincinnati, OH: Raisbeck & Company, 1914), no pagination.
147. Grebner, *We Were the Ninth*, 135.
148. Max Burgheim, *Police and Municipal Guide* (Cincinnati: Ohio Book Store, 1995), 32.

149. Gollmer, *Namenlisten der Pioneere*, 22.
150. *Cincinnati Volksblatt*, June 22, 1889, 11.
151. *Cincinnati Volksblatt*, May 31, 1889.
152. *Cincinnati Volksfreund*, December 1872.
153. *Cincinnati Volksfreund*, August 2, 1872.
154. *Cincinnati Volksblatt*, August 8, 1884, 4.
155. *Cincinnati Freie Presse*, December 25, 1883.
156. *Northside Transcript*, March 15, 1879.
157. *Northside Transcript*, February 14, 1880.
158. *Cincinnati Volksblatt*, July 7, 1884.
159. LDS Microfilm #0069434, Penzlin, Mecklenburg Church Records, 1774–1840, Church of Jesus Christ of Latter-Day Saints Family History Library, Salt Lake City, Utah.
160. Grebner, *We Were the Ninth*, 17.
161. Siegfried Heuer, *Chronik der Stadt Penzlin* (Neubrandenburg, Mecklenburg-Vorpommern: Heinz Walthe, 2001), 51.
162. Williams City Directories, Cincinnati, Ohio, 1859–80.
163. Heuer, *Chronik der Stadt Penzlin*, 62, 83.
164. Wolffradt and Damus, *Turnfest-führer*, 184, 202, 204.
165. Burgheim, *Cincinnati im Wort und Bild*, 369–70.
166. Ibid., 488.
167. *Dayton Daily Journal*, October 31, 1908.
168. *Turner Normal College Alumni Bulletin* (Indianapolis, IN: Turner Normal College, May 1932), 15.
169. *Illinois v. August Spies et al.*, trial transcript no. 1, "Affidavits of John Phillip Deluse, Jacob L. Biehler and Oscar Sputh, 1886 Oct. 1–1886 Oct. 7."
170. 1898 Roster of Members Combined GAR Posts (Cohen and Company Printers, September 1, 1898), 51.
171. Ibid.
172. Ibid.
173. Burgheim, *Cincinnati im Wort und Bild*, 436.
174. Burgheim, *Police and Municipal Guide*, 58.
175. *Northside Transcript*, 1877.
176. *Northside Transcript*, June 22, 1889.
177. *Northside Transcript*, January 18, 1890.
178. *Northside Transcript*, April 13, 1889.
179. Souvenir History of Cumminsville, 1914.

Chapter 6

180. *Silver Jubilee: Grand Exhibition, Ball Park, June 16, Outing and Exhibition, June 17* (Cincinnati, OH: Roessler Brothers, 1906), 13.
181. Ibid., 14.
182. Ibid., 15.
183. Ibid.
184. *New York Times*, June 24, 1885.
185. Max Monte, *Souvenir zu der einweihungsfeier der halle des Nord Cincinnati Turnvereins: Sonntag, 26, November, 1893* (Cincinnati, OH: Weier and Daiker, Printers, 1893), 41.
186. *Silver Jubilee*, 16.
187. Monte, *Souvenir zu der einweihungsfeier*, 4.
188. Adolph Varrelman, *North Cincinnati Gym News* 4, no. 7 (May 1918): 4.
189. *The Playground* (April 1917): 240. Published monthly at Cooperstown, New York, for the Playground and Recreation Commission of America.
190. *Silver Jubilee*, 21.
191. *Vorstand des NCTV, Nord Cincinnati Turnverein Fest Program* (New York: Allied Printing, 1910).
192. Adolph Varrelman, "Save the Zoo," *North Cincinnati Gym News* 5, no. 5 (March 1919): 7.
193. *North Cincinnati Gym News* 4, no. 7 (May 1918): 1.
194. *North Cincinnati Gym News* 4, no. 8 (May 1918): 6.
195. *North Cincinnati Gym News* 4, no. 8 (June 1918): 4.
196. Ibid.
197. Ibid.
198. Ibid.
199. *North Cincinnati Gym News* 4, no. 11 (September 1918): 4–5.
200. *North Cincinnati Gym News* 4, no. 8 (June 1918): 1.
201. *North Cincinnati Turner Leben* 3, no. 12 (October 1917): 1.
202. *North Cincinnati Gym News* 4, no. 11 (September 1918): 6.
203. *North Cincinnati Gym News* 4, no. 8 (June 1918): 6.
204. August Gary Hermann Papers 1877–1938, Box 8, Folder 19, Baseball Hall of Fame Archives, Cooperstown, New York.
205. *Cincinnati Enquirer*, September 11, 1886, 16.
206. Burgheim, *Cincinnati im Wort und Bild*, 501.
207. Doscher's French Chewy Taffy, http://www.frenchchewcandy.com/#history.
208. *Silver Jubilee*, 35.

209. Ibid., 49.
210. *North Cincinnati Turner Leben* 3, no. 12 (October 1917): 8.
211. Certificates of Honor for the Wright Brothers, Orville and Wilbur, from the Nord Cincinnati Turnverein, MS-1, Box 44, Items 5 and 6, Wright State University Libraries Special Collection, Dayton, Ohio.
212. *North Cincinnati Gym News* 4, no. 7 (May 1918): 5.
213. *Silver Jubilee*, 35.
214. Ibid.
215. Ibid., 50.
216. Ibid., 51.
217. *Cincinnati Volksblatt*, June 21, 1889, 11.
218. Ibid.
219. *Columbus Citizen*, March 9, 1901, 5.
220. Burgheim, *Cincinnati im Wort und Bild*, 310.
221. Ibid.
222. Records of the Cincinnati Baseball Club Archival Collection, Cincinnati Historical Society, Cincinnati, Ohio.

Chapter 7

223. Dobling, *Diamond Jubilee Pageant*, 15.
224. Ibid., 17.
225. Ibid.
226. Ibid.
227. Ibid., 21.
228. Ibid., 37.
229. *Kentucky Post*, December 13, 1915.
230. Dobling, *Diamond Jubilee Pageant*, 21–22.
231. *The Gymnast* 5, no. 10 (June 1927): 1–2.
232. Dobling, *Diamond Jubilee Pageant*, 11–13.
233. *Kentucky Post*, October 15, 1931, 10.
234. *Kentucky Post*, February 12, 1932, 1.
235. Covington Turners, *Diamond Jubilee Souvenir Book*, 5.
236. Ibid., 11.
237. Ibid., 11–12.
238. Kenton County, Kentucky Historical Society, *Northern Kentucky History* 7, no. 2 (Spring–Summer 2000): 41.
239. Covington Turners, *Diamond Jubilee Souvenir Book*, 29–30.

240. Kenton County, Kentucky Historical Society, *Northern Kentucky History* 7, no. 2 (Spring–Summer 2000): 41.
241. Covington Turners, *Diamond Jubilee Souvenir Book*, 19.
242. Burgheim, *Cincinnati im Wort und Bild*, 541.
243. Kenton County, Kentucky Historical Society, *Northern Kentucky History* 7, no. 2 (Spring–Summer 2000): 24–25.
244. Ibid.
245. Ibid.
246. *Cincinnati Enquirer*, Wednesday, August 28, 2002.
247. Kenton County, Kentucky Historical Society, *Northern Kentucky History* 7, no. 2 (Spring–Summer 2000): 41.
248. Ibid., 42.
249. *Newport Local*, April 24, 1877.
250. *Newport Local*, November 22, 1877.
251. *Newport Local*, December 8, 1877, 3.
252. *Kentucky State Journal*, May 22, 1884, 5.
253. Covington Turners, *Diamond Jubilee Souvenir Book*, 15.

CHAPTER 8

254. Dayton Turners Association, *Seventy-fifth Anniversary Banquet Program* (Dayton, Ohio, 1928), 7.
255. Ibid., 11.
256. Curt Dalton, *The Breweries of Dayton: An Illustrated History* (Dayton, OH: Montgomery County Historical Society Publishing, 1995), 47.
257. Karl Karlstaedt, *In Commemoration of the Golden Jubilee of the German Pioneer Society* (Dayton, OH: Greater Dayton Gazette Company, 1928), 39.
258. *Dayton Daily News*, Wednesday, July 2, 2003.
259. Dayton Turners Association, *Seventy-fifth Anniversary Banquet Program*, 4.
260. Betty Dietz Krebs, "Happy Anniversary—Dayton Liederkranz Turner Society Celebrates 100 Years with Concert," *Dayton Daily News*, Thursday, October 25, 1990.
261. Alta Harvey Heiser, *Hamilton in the Making* (Oxford, OH: Mississippi Valley Press, 1941), 222–23.
262. Nicholas Longworth, Letter to the Editors, *Cincinnati Gazette*, 1850.
263. *Cincinnati Volksblatt*, July 7, 1884.
264. Gary Lind, *Our Sesquicentennial 1851–2001, Martini United Church of Christ* (Cincinnati, Ohio, n.d.), 7–8.

265. Burgheim, *Cincinnati im Wort und Bild*, 517.
266. Ibid.
267. American Turner Records, National Council Reports, 1905–1938, Ruth Lily Special Collections and Archives, University Library, Purdue University, Indianapolis, Indiana.
268. Covington Turners, *Diamond Jubilee Souvenir Book*, 23.
269. American Turner Records, National Council Reports, 1907.
270. Margaret Guentert, *Norwood Ohio: A Bicentennial Remembrance* (Cincinnati, OH: Allis Chalmers Inc., 1976), 95–96.
271. Ibid., 97–98.
272. Ibid., 99–100.

Chapter 9

273. Don Heinrich Tolzmann, *German-American Literature* (Metuchen, NJ: Scarecrow Press, Inc., 1977), 274.
274. *Eightieth Annual Report of the Public Schools of Cincinnati for the School Year Ending August 31, 1909* (Cincinnati, OH: Cincinnati School Board, 1909).
275. *Eightieth Annual Report*, 510.
276. Ibid., 282.
277. Ibid., 283.
278. Ibid., 284.
279. *North Cincinnati Gym News* 4, no. 7 (May 1918): 2.
280. *Eightieth Annual Report*, 286.
281. John Brough Shotwell, *A History of the Schools of Cincinnati* (Cincinnati, OH: School Life Company, 1900), 101.
282. John J. Molter, Civic Leader, posted note to sanduskyhistory.blogspot.com on Wednesday, June 13, 2010, Sandusky Library Archives Research Center.
283. *Eightieth Annual Report*, 286–87.
284. Shotwell, *History of the Schools*, 103–4.
285. *North Cincinnati Gym News* 4, no. 12 (October 1918): 8.
286. *North Cincinnati Turner Leben* 4, no. 3 (January 1918): 4.
287. *American Turner Topics* 1, no. 8, "Honor to Whom Is Due!" (March 1937). Pittsburgh, Pennsylvania.
288. Burgheim, *Cincinnati im Wort und Bild*, 433.
289. Ohio District Turners, *Symposium of Papers*, 11.
290. Cincinnati Central Turners, *The First Hundred Years 1848–1949* (Cincinnati, Ohio, 1948), 22.

291. *North Cincinnati Gym News* 4, no. 7 (May 1918): 2.
292. Cincinnati Central Turner Records, Meeting Minutes, 1848–61.
293. Cincinnati Central Turners, *First Hundred Years*, 27.
294. George Seibel, ed., *Turner Topics* 2, no. 4 (November 1937): 3. Pittsburgh, Pennsylvania.
295. Shotwell, *History of the Schools*, 104.
296. Ibid., 104–5.
297. David M. Jordan, *Pete Rose: A Biography* (Westport, CT: Greenwood Press, 2004), 6.
298. *American Turner Topics*, “These Pioneers: A Tribute to Three Leaders in Physical Education Who Have Helped Develop Sound Bodies for 50 Years” (September 1940), Pittsburgh, Pennsylvania.
299. Cincinnati Central Turners, *First Hundred Years*, 27.
300. Cincinnati Central Turners, *Sesquicentennial Celebration, August 1, 1998.*

About the Author

Dann Woellert enjoys living the Turner principle of a "sound mind in a sound body." An avid kayaker, hiker and practitioner of anusara yoga, he is a self-proclaimed history geek and creator and guide of the Northside/Cumminsville Historical Architectural Tour for the Cincinnati Architreks. He is also author of *Cincinnati's Northside Neighborhood* (2009). Dann lives in Hyde Park in Cincinnati, Ohio, but enjoys spending time in the original Cincinnati Turner neighborhood, Over-the-Rhine.